New Directions for
Higher Education

Betsy O. Barefoot
Jillian L. Kinzie
CO-EDITORS

Codes of Conduct in Academia

John M. Braxton
Nathaniel J. Bray
EDITORS

Number 160 • Winter 2012
Jossey-Bass
San Francisco

CODES OF CONDUCT IN ACADEMIA
John M. Braxton, Nathaniel J. Bray
New Directions for Higher Education, no. 160
Betsy O. Barefoot and Jillian L. Kinzie, Co-editors

Microfilm copies of issues and articles are available in 16mm and 35mm, as well as microfiche in 105mm, through University Microfilms Inc., 300 North Zeeb Road, Ann Arbor, MI 48106-1346.

NEW DIRECTIONS FOR HIGHER EDUCATION (ISSN 0271-0560, electronic ISSN 1536-0741) is part of The Jossey-Bass Higher and Adult Education Series and is published quarterly by Wiley Subscription Services, Inc., A Wiley Company, at Jossey-Bass, One Montgomery Street, Suite 1200, San Francisco, CA 94104-4594. Periodicals Postage Paid at San Francisco, California, and at additional mailing offices. POSTMASTER: Send address changes to New Directions for Higher Education, Jossey-Bass, One Montgomery Street, Suite 1200, San Francisco, CA 94104-4594.

New Directions for Higher Education is indexed in Current Index to Journals in Education (ERIC); Higher Education Abstracts.

Individual subscription rate (in USD): $89 per year US/Can/Mex, $113 rest of world; institutional subscription rate: $292 US, $332 Can/Mex, $366 rest of world. Single copy rate: $29. Electronic only–all regions: $89 individual, $292 institutional; Print & Electronic–US: $98 individual, $335 institutional; Print & Electronic–Canada/Mexico: $98 individual, $375 institutional; Print & Electronic–Rest of World: $122 individual, $409 institutional.

Editorial correspondence should be sent to the Co-editor, Betsy O. Barefoot, Gardner Institute, Box 72, Brevard, NC 28712.

Cover photograph © Digital Vision

www.josseybass.com

CONTENTS

1

This chapter emphasizes the importance of codes of conduct to guide the professional role performance of presidents, academic deans, admissions officers, fund-raising professionals, and faculty who teach undergraduate and graduate students.

Introduction: The Importance of Codes of Conduct for Academia

John M. Braxton, Nathaniel J. Bray

Colleges and universities function as client-serving organizations (Baldridge et al. 1978). The clients served range from prospective donors, prospective students, the individual college or university, faculty members, students as groups, and students as individuals to the knowledge base of the various academic disciplines (Braxton 2010).

Such critical role positions as the presidency, the academic deanship, admissions officers, institutional advancement officers, and faculty members serve one or more of these various clients (Braxton 2010). The occupants of such critical role positions experience role ambiguity or substantial autonomy in the performance of their roles. For example, Birnbaum and Eckel (2005) posit that presidents experience role ambiguity and uncertainty over the way their roles should be performed. Likewise Wolverton, Wolverton, and Gmelch (1999) contend that academic deans also experience role ambiguity and uncertainty. College admissions officers (Hodum and James 2010), institutional advancement officers (Caboni 2010), and college and university faculty members possess considerable autonomy in the performance of their respective roles in both undergraduate teaching (Braxton and Bayer 1999) and graduate teaching and mentoring (Braxton, Proper, and Bayer 2011).

Both role ambiguity and role autonomy strongly indicate the need for formal or informal codes of conduct to protect the welfare of the various clients served by these critical role positions (Braxton 2010). Without the existence of formal or informal codes of conduct to provide guidelines for the performance of these roles, college presidents, academic deans, admissions officers, institutional advancement officers, and individual college and university faculty members are free to make unconstrained and idiosyncratic choices in the performance of their respective roles (Braxton 2010).

NEW DIRECTIONS FOR HIGHER EDUCATION, no. 160, Winter 2012 © Wiley Periodicals, Inc.
Published online in Wiley Online Library (wileyonlinelibrary.com) • DOI:10.1002/he.20031

In addition to providing parameters for the professional choices of individuals in critical role positions in higher education, codes of conduct also assist the academy in professional self-regulation. William Goode (1969) asserts that the lay public grants professions autonomy in exchange for professional self-regulation. Professional self-regulation entails the exercise of social control of wrongdoing through the deterrence, detection, and sanctioning of professional impropriety (Zuckerman 1988). Codes of conduct play a key part in these three mechanisms of social control.

Accordingly, this issue of *New Directions for Higher Education* focuses on two key issues regarding codes of conduct: the construction of codes of conduct and the existence of codes of conduct in academia. Five chapters of this issue propose tenets for the construction of codes of conduct for such critical role positions as the presidency, the academic deanship, admissions officers, institutional advancement officers, and the graduate teaching and mentoring role of university faculty members. The tenets advanced by each of these chapters rest on a robust foundation of empirically derived normative structures for these critical roles. Norms are shared beliefs of a particular social or professional group that focus on expected or desired behaviors in various professional situations and circumstances (Gibbs 1981; Rossi and Berk 1985). Further clarity comes from Merton's definition of norms as prescribed or proscribed patterns of behavior (Merton 1968, 1973).

These five chapters are as follows. In chapter 2, titled "Toward a Code of Conduct for the Presidency," J. Christopher Fleming, proposes eight tenets for a code of conduct for the presidency of colleges and universities. Such a code of conduct safeguards the welfare of clients both external and internal to the president's college or university. Nathaniel J. Bray describes six tenets for academic deans in the third chapter, which bears the title "Follow the Code: Rules or Guidelines for Academic Deans' Behavior?" The clients affected by the role performance of academic deans include the institution, the academic college, and the faculty (Braxton 2010). In the fourth chapter titled "A Normative Code of Conduct for Admissions Officers," Robert L. Hodum delineates nine tenets toward a code of conduct for college and university admissions officers. Such a proposed code protects the welfare of such clients as the prospective student, the parents of prospective students, and the institution of employment. In the fifth chapter, Timothy C. Caboni discerns nine tenets for a code of conduct for institutional advancement officers. Such a code of conduct safeguards the welfare of such clients as the donor and the institution. The title of his chapter is "College and University Codes of Conduct for Fund-Raising Professionals." In the last of this set of five chapters, Eve Proper outlines six tenets of a possible code of conduct for graduate faculty members to guide them in teaching and mentoring graduate students. The title of this sixth chapter is "Toward a Code of Conduct for Graduate Education." The tenets described by Proper shelter the welfare of such diverse clients as graduate students, the institution, and academic disciplines.

NEW DIRECTIONS FOR HIGHER EDUCATION • DOI:10.1002/he

As previously indicated, the existence of codes of conduct constitutes another issue addressed by this volume. In chapter 7, Dawn Lyken-Segosebe, Yunkyung Min, and John M. Braxton report the findings of study conducted to determine if codes of conduct for undergraduate college teaching exist in teaching-oriented colleges and universities. The title of their chapter is aptly labeled "The Existence of Codes of Conduct for Undergraduate Teaching in Teaching-Oriented Four-Year Colleges and Universities."

In addition to the construction and existence of codes of conduct, this volume would be incomplete without a thorough discussion of the various issues colleges and universities as organization face in adopting codes of conduct. Nathaniel J. Bray, Danielle K. Molina, and Bart A. Swecker present a thorough consideration of such related topics as the rationale for ethical codes, an overview of the organizational principles underlying their development and functioning, the ways in which ethical codes function as organizational anchors for key constituent groups in higher education, the constraints of institutional structures, and the possibilities for the development of codes of conduct in higher education. The title of this eighth chapter is "Organizational Constraints and Possibilities Regarding Codes of Conduct."

The last chapter of this volume is titled "Reflections on Codes of Conduct: Asymmetries, Vulnerabilities, and Institutional Controls" and is written by Nathaniel J. Bray and John M. Braxton. This final chapter focuses upon trends seen in the empirically derived codes of conduct that have been developed to this point. They present a detailed consideration of the asymmetries that exist in both positional and professional authority, the relations between main campus stakeholders, and the vulnerabilities that are presented by power differentials in both schemata. The work concludes with a discussion of the detection, sanctioning, and deterrence of normative violations.

References

Baldridge, J., D. Curtis, G. Ecker, and G. Riley. 1978. *Policy Making and Effective Leadership*. San Francisco: Jossey-Bass.

Birnbaum, R., and P. D. Eckel. 2005. "The Dilemma of Presidential Leadership." In *American Higher Education in the Twenty First Century: Social, Political, and Economic Challenges*, edited by P. G. Altbach, R. O. Berdahl, and P. J. Gumport. Baltimore: Johns Hopkins University Press.

Braxton, J. 2010. "Norms and the Work of Colleges and Universities: Introduction to the Special Issue-Norms in Academia." *Journal of Higher Education* 81(3): 243–250.

Braxton, J. M., and A. E. Bayer. 1999. *Faculty Misconduct in Collegiate Teaching*. Baltimore: Johns Hopkins University Press.

Braxton, J. M., E. Proper, and A. E. Bayer. 2011. *Professors Behaving Badly: Faculty Misconduct in Graduate Education*. Baltimore: Johns Hopkins University Press.

Caboni, T. C. 2010. "The Normative Structure of College and University Fundraising Behaviors." *Journal of Higher Education* 81(3): 339–365.

Gibbs, J. 1981. *Norms, Deviance, and Social Control: Conceptual Matters.* New York: Elsevier.

Goode, W. 1969. "The Theoretical Limits of Professionalization." In *The Semi-Professions and Their Organization*, edited by A. Etzioni. New York: Free Press.

Hodum, R. L., and G. W. James. 2010. "An Observation of Normative Structure for Colleges Admission and Recruitment Officers." *Journal of Higher Education* 81(3): 317–338.

Merton, R. 1968. *Social Theory and Social Structure.* New York: Free Press.

Merton, R. 1973. *The Sociology of Science: Theoretical and Empirical Investigations.* Chicago: University of Chicago Press.

Rossi, P., and R. Berk. 1985. "Varieties of Normative Consensus." *American Sociological Review* 50(3): 333–347.

Wolverton, M., M. L. Wolverton, and W. H. Gmelch. 1999. "The Impact of Role Conflict and Ambiguity on Academic Deans." *Journal of Higher Education* 70(1): 80–106.

Zuckerman, H. 1988. "The Sociology of Science." In *Handbook of Sociology*, edited by N. Smelser. Thousand Oaks, CA: Sage Publications.

JOHN M. BRAXTON *is professor of education in the Higher Education Leadership and Policy Program at Peabody College of Vanderbilt University. Professor Braxton's scholarly interests include social control in academia with a particular focus on codes of conduct; norms; and the deterrence, detection, and sanctioning of violations of codes and norms.*

NATHANIEL J. BRAY *is an associate professor and program coordinator in Higher Education Administration at the University of Alabama. His research interests include normative structures for academic administrators, sociology of higher education, and student issues across higher education.*

NEW DIRECTIONS FOR HIGHER EDUCATION • DOI:10.1002/he

2

College and university presidents serve clients who are internal and external to their institution. This chapter describes eight tenets toward a code of conduct for college and university presidents that safeguards the welfare of the clients served.

Toward a Code of Conduct for the Presidency

J. Christopher Fleming

The cooperative engagement between college presidents and faculty is germane to the cultivation of healthy associations between the faculty and institutional governing boards. This cyclical relationship between president, faculty, and the board is a critical element in sustaining institutional productivity and efficacy (Association of Governing Boards of Universities and Colleges 2009). However, the continuous evolution of American postsecondary institutions has fostered questions regarding the changing ethos of the academy, which has challenged the traditional notion of the community of students and scholars and intertwined the academy's customary paradigms of governance with the principles of business (Lachs 2011).

Academic culture and governance of the academy are maintained through the balance of the shared governance structures. Presidents occupy a central position in maintaining the stability of the governance arrangement. Faculty share in the decision-making processes of the academy (Johnston 2003), manage the legitimacy of the president (Bensimon 1991), and maintain oversight of administration's compliance with the institution's mission and values (Bornstein 2003; Bray 2003; Olscamp 2003). However, American colleges and universities are changing and as a result so are their presidents.

The chronicled history of higher education provides testimony to the professional evolution of the college and university president as the office has matured into the academy's public face and the principal decision-making locus within the modern postsecondary institutional structure. Although the academy presidency has been in existence for centuries (Prator 1963), the highest executive position on American college and university campuses remains ambiguous and a managerial enigma.

New Directions for Higher Education, no. 160, Winter 2012 © Wiley Periodicals, Inc.
Published online in Wiley Online Library (wileyonlinelibrary.com) • DOI:10.1002/he.20032

The lack of understanding regarding the office of president is perplexing and has brought about many of the misunderstandings attributed to the campus' chief executive office. Challenges concerning the president's importance and role (Ward 2002) have been abundant (Birnbaum 1989). However, despite the criticisms and inquiries of purpose, the academy presidency has endured and emerged as a key role in the promotion and communication of the institutional mission (Birnbaum 2002) and the public reflection of the academy's character and values (Romesburg 2010). Prator (1963, 27) notes, "No person on the college campus is more nearly the interpreter of the philosophy of the campus than is the president."

Decades after Prator's observation, the role of the president as the institutional values bearer continues to hold true. The Association of Governing Boards reports, "In public venues, a president's words and actions almost always are taken as expressions of the institution's identity" (Romesburg 2010, 2). Time and research have revealed that the academy president is a pivotal herald within the higher education hierarchy. Because presidents are the chief institutional spokesperson (Balderston 1995) and the symbolic representation of the academy, it stands to reason that they become the target for so much criticism (Dennison 2001; Romesburg 2010).

Concerns regarding alleged improprieties have not always been an inherent trait associated with postsecondary institution chief executive officers. Dennison (2001, 269) declares that the admiration of modern university presidents has diminished. Long gone is the "warm glow of admiring public opinion; fifty years earlier real giants ruled the campuses." Walker (1981) explains that behavioral improprieties are not consistently brought to light within the academic community. Across higher education institutions there are standardized norms that dictate capitulation to specific academic values and guidelines. However, modern academy presidents have received increased attention due to their public nature and prominent community engagement.

Despite the frequency of purported inappropriate behavior concerning administrative firings and reclassifications of staff (Stripling 2012); moral misconduct (McGill, Assad, and Sheehan 2011; Van Der Werf 1999); malfeasance (Welte 2003); financial mismanagement (Rogers and Tresaugue 2008); disregard of the principle of academic values (Lester 2010); unbecoming behavior (Fain 2008; Guess 2007); and failure to maintain proper autonomy and shared governance principles (Hebel 2012; Masterson 2009) by academy presidents, the number of higher education institutions that have developed a code of ethics for their presidents continues to be few (Fleming 2010). Varying implicit organizational theories conflict with the conceptual ideals institutional constituencies have of the organization's purpose (Birnbaum 1988; Boschken 1994). The cacophony of dueling ideologies originates from individual or association interests of institutional enclaves and perpetuates the conceptual ambiguity inherent in the roles of the academy presidency (Neumann and Bensimon 1990).

In his historical narrative of American higher education, Prator (1963) traces the evolutionary development of colleges and universities to the newly developed colonial states. Although the president functions as the chief envoy of the institution (Balderston 1995), the occupant of the office of president must be skillful at developing and cultivating domestic relationships and peripheral associations vital to the academy's systemic and strategic success. Colleges and universities are social institutions (Cohen and March 1974) that maintain a social culture regulating the interactions of their constituencies. As the chief executive officer, the president is a predominant figure in the advancement and communication of the institutional narrative, it is his or her responsibility to bring together assorted and divergent perspectives and ideologies.

By cultivating relationships with the institution's various constituencies, the president navigates numerous expectations and works to engender support (Koch and Fisher 1996). Bornstein (2003) states that the lack of a congruent relationship with internal and external institutional constituents reduces the president's ability to establish legitimacy and support. Although presidents have numerous groups and associations vying for their support and attention, it is important to note that the president–faculty relationship is pivotal to establishing legitimacy and institutional success. Relationship management encourages avenues through which reciprocal communication may take place. The social construct of congruent relationships defines participant roles, establishes balance and value, and inspires continuous engagement for the eventual benefit of all (Wettersten and Lichtenberg 1995). As coalition builders, academy presidents must engage faculty, staff, students, alumni, boards, donors, and other community associations. Inherent within the president's duties is the construction of mutually beneficial partnerships that enable the institution to bolster its academic reputation, increase its endowments, and expand its reach within the areas of research and service.

Fain (2006) argued that the most common obstacles to presidential success are the relationships that are nonexistent or underdeveloped. Bornstein (2003) accentuates the significance of relationship building in stipulating that the legitimacy of the college and university president remains correlated to the president's ability to develop internal relationships, specifically with the faculty. Other scholars concur that the initiation and cultivation of relationships between presidents and their numerous and various constituencies are essential not only to the success of the president but also to the prosperity of the institution (Michael, Schwartz, and Balraj 2001; Olscamp 2003).

The construct of relationship building predicates that postsecondary institutions function within social interactional webs. In this particular case, academy presidents are centrally located within the organization's social web of interactions. Due to the connectivity of the relational network, the behaviors demonstrated by the president reverberate throughout the entire organization. According to Wettersten and Lichtenberg (1995), relationship development is established on the mutual contextual constructs of the association and the delineation of roles within the interaction. President–constituency relationships should be established on clearly prescribed, mutually agreed-upon expectations and role responsibilities. The adherence to these established relational expectations cultivates interactions that are congruent and satisfying to each of the participants involved. The results of relational congruency stimulate clarity of expectations, interactive boundaries, and role performance.

The president–faculty relationship holds particular significance, as it is this relationship that serves as a barometer of presidential legitimacy and support within the academy constituency (Bensimon 1991; Birnbaum 1992; Bornstein 2003). Davis and Davis (1999) explain that postsecondary faculty occupy a strategic position within the academy structure: engaging the president and other institutional administrators in decisions concerning matters within the faculty purview.

Expectations concerning the normative pattern of behaviors are an intrinsic standard within professional and social groups, such as the professoriate (Braxton 2010). As the vast majority of academy presidents have emerged from the faculty ranks, the professoriate promulgates a certain code of ethics that must be clearly defined and articulated. Recent changes outlined in the demographic portrait of college and university presidents (American Council on Education 2012) reveal an increased percentage of nonacademic candidates ascending to the highest levels of leadership within colleges and universities. In addition, this report corroborates the fact that academy presidents continue to cite problematic areas such as faculty relations and the ambiguity of the presidential office. Increases in the number of college presidents arriving from outside the academy require that guidelines regulating the role performance of the presidency be clearly delineated and understood.

Recent research analysis focuses particular consideration on the significant internal relationships academy presidents must have with the professoriate. Current literature reveals that college and university faculty may exert significant influence on the level of presidential support and serve as key partners in the president's vision (Fleming 2010). In addition, president–faculty relationships have been found to have a direct correlation to the welfare of the institution (Michael, Schwartz, and Balraj 2001; Olscamp 2003) and the chief executive officer's ability to lead and manage successfully (Bensimon 1991). Although the importance of this dyadic relationship is unquestioned, the fact remains that little has been done to codify the president–faculty relationship in order to enhance its congruency.

Tenets for a Code of Conduct

Thus, it is important that institutions develop a prescribed code of ethics that addresses the faculty's expectations of presidential role performance. It is inevitable that in discussing the president–faculty relationship, one should consider the president's orientation of service to this governance constituency group. In expanding the application of the orientation of service and the correlation of president–faculty relational congruency, I propose eight precepts as an institutional code of conduct for academy presidents to incorporate. These tenets are extrapolated from Fleming's (2010) description of the empirically derived proscriptive norms that regulate presidential role performance. These empirically derived norms (identified in the following paragraphs in *italics*) provide a basis for the generation of a code of conduct that represents a faculty-centered perspective of the role performance of academy presidents. As a result, the tenets identified in this presidential code of conduct are not exhaustive. Variance in institutional mission, values, expectations, academic scope, social environment, and group affiliation may retract or expand the need for broader or a more narrowly tailored code of presidential conduct. However, these tenets should serve as a foundation of rudimentary expectations for any college or university president.

Tenet One. Presidential boundaries must be clearly identified and articulated. Presidents must have functional knowledge of institutional regulations, state and federal laws, and accreditation association rules and be adept at applying them universally. The authority of the office and the extent to which the college and university president may invoke executive privilege must be prescribed from the beginning. A canon of presidential authority should be provided during the presidential selection process. As each institution is different in its mission, values, and focus; so should the canons of presidential authority vary to meet the scope and mission of each individual institution. However, certain principles should be standard regardless of institution type and affiliation. The normative patterns of *Anonymous Privilege* and *Philosophical Isolation* empirically identified by Fleming provide support for this tenet. The norm of *Anonymous Privilege* condemns indulgence in actions that insinuate special presidential privileges that have not been officially sanctioned as appropriate or officially prescribed, and *Philosophical Isolation* denounces segregated attitudes vis-à-vis organizational management and institutional decision making (Fleming 2010).

Tenet Two. Presidents must maintain open communication and social engagement in the community and with critical industry partners involved in relationship building for the institution. Frequent and substantive interactions with various community and corporate partners should become a routine occurrence allowing for a multidirectional exchange of ideas. The foundation of this tenet is grounded in the normative patterns of *Debilitating Diplomacy* and *Differential Communications* (Fleming 2010). Behaviors categorized under the normative pattern of *Debilitating Diplomacy* reflect presidential behavior that engages individuals and groups in such a fashion as to cause alienation and ill will. *Differential Communication* essentially represents presidential behaviors that lack the fundamental communication needed to keep institutional constituencies properly informed. These behaviors may also include the dissemination of misinformation.

Tenet Three. Academy presidents must demonstrate and encourage open-mindedness, unbiased dialogue, and the notion of cooperation and teamwork (Fleming 2010). The president must be adept at the art of collaboration (McGoey 2007) and possess the ability to influence people through the building of coalitions and dialogue. The normative pattern of *Homogeneous Reflection* supports the principle of this tenet and censures the occurrence of obtuse decision making, ideological isolation, actions that work against coalition building, and a president's inability to represent his or her constituencies (Fleming 2010).

Understanding the interactions that develop within a social organization requires a framework through which organizations and their emerging associations can be understood. Bolman and Deal (1997) propose four categorical frames for understanding social organizations such as colleges and universities; each frame addresses a variant perception of understanding the way in which the academy operates internally and with the external community in which it exists. The "structural frame" examines the infrastructure of the organization and places special emphasis on the formal associations, roles, and the use of technology in the organization. The specific objective of this frame is to demonstrate how the lack of fit in organizational structure can hinder the efficiency and effectiveness of leadership and the institution. The "human resource frame" personifies the organization's varied opinions and ideas. Through this frame, the academy is regarded as a learning entity with an understanding of change and a desire to defend traditional academic canons. The "political frame" interprets the academy as a dynamic system with competing interests and limited resources. In this frame, participants and coalitions are fluid and change is the prevailing norm. The "symbolic frame" demonstrates the values and the image the academy reflects as a cultural institution. The academy is an organization guided by policies, tradition, rituals, and institutional stories.

Tenet Four. The chief executive officer of any institution should have an eclectic perception of how the academy functions within varied conceptual frames. Presidents who are one dimensional are plagued with perceived or actual ignorance of community needs and find their ability to lead riddled with criticisms and disdain. Presidents must demonstrate a functional knowledge of the academy's role in the community and have the ability to articulate the economic and social benefits the institution brings to the local and, in some respects, the global society.

The normative patterns of *Inattentive Representation* and *Negative Symbolism* (Fleming 2010) address the president's inability to effectively represent the core values and institutional culture of the academy and its community. *Inattentive Representation* relates to the president's inability to engage in active fund-raising, lack of engagement with the external community, and failure to articulate the needs and concerns of the faculty and other institutional constituencies to the dominant coalition. *Negative symbolism* reflects a president's inability to personify the values of the institution and the practice of engaging in behaviors that reflect negatively on the institution and the community as a whole.

The role of the institution and how the institutional culture complements the external community are key aspects. Frequent town hall assemblies and other social interactions with varying segments of the institution's external community should be a routine occurrence for the president. Certainly, these interactions should be a customary practice for new presidents but these interactions should extend throughout the president's tenure. Research focused on presidential effectiveness in higher education identified the president's ability to have healthy relationships with important constituencies as a key trait that facilitates the acquisition of resources and maintains presidential credibility (McGoey 2007).

Financial reductions, competition for limited resources, and fluid political participants have propelled fund-raising activities to one of the most fundamental responsibilities for modern college and university presidents. Bornstein (2003) catalogs the role of the president into four primary areas of responsibility: academic, managerial, financial, and external. The fiduciary role of the president (also addressed in Tenet Six) encapsulates the president's fund-raising and stewardship of the institution's limited resources. The acquisition of resources directly affects the welfare of the faculty and the institution as a whole. Increased funding and resource acquisition can stimulate institutional growth and enhance the academic footprint of the institution. Through the principles of shared governance, academy faculties have the responsibility of monitoring the behavior of institutional administrators (Bray 2003). The fashion in which the president represents the institution and the results of his or her engagement may enhance or reduce the president's ability to lead and the ultimate success of the institution (Bornstein 2003).

Tenet Five. Sexual or other inappropriate actions that call into question the morality of the president are highly prohibited and presidents should abstain from these behaviors. The normative patterns of *Moral Turpitude and Professional Disregard* (Fleming 2010) denote disdain for presidents involved in these types of inappropriate behaviors. Presidents should not engage in behaviors that offend institutional values and conflict with morals of the collective society. Romantic involvement with students and subordinate staff members is considered behavior unbecoming a president (Fleming 2010). The norm of *Professional Disregard* speaks to the president's lack of professional responsibility and adherence to institutional rules and policies and involves situations that call into question the president's ethics.

Tenet Six. Presidents occupy numerous roles and must be skilled at the acquisition of resources for the institution. Institutional resources must be secured and disseminated in an honest and transparent fashion. The normative pattern of *Fiduciary Irresponsibility* (Fleming 2010) explores presidential behaviors that demonstrate the imprudent acquisition, designation, and stewardship of financial resources. A blatant disregard for the wishes of donors and the use of institutional funds contrary to their intended purpose are also behaviors that embody this normative pattern.

Tenet Seven. Presidents must acknowledge and adhere to the traditional norms of the academy. They must demonstrate an ability to lead and manage without being perceived as intrusive or divisive. The normative pattern of *Intrusive Manipulation* demonstrates a violation of role designation and diminishes the traditional purviews of the faculty. Presidential interference in grade assessment decisions and course content decisions demonstrates a violation of this normative pattern.

Tenet Eight. College and university presidents should cultivate an inclusive decision-making process and demonstrate dedication to the needs of their constituencies. An understanding of the institutional needs and a dedication to the mission and vision of the institution encourage the allegiance of the faculty, staff, students, and the community as a whole. The normative pattern of *Constituency Insensitivity* addresses presidential behavior that neglects the concerns or issues of the institution's constituencies. This disregard for constituency concerns may manifest in clear disregard or blatant inaction. The normative pattern of *Unrequited Concern* focuses on the lack of empathy and consideration given to constituency concerns during decision-making processes. Behaviors that demonstrate unrequited concern include the president's ignoring of faculty input on academic issues, unilateral decision making that excludes key participants, and acts of retribution that include lack of funding or resources for departments that disagree with the president's academic philosophy.

Further support for these eight tenets comes from Moore's three principles that comprise the orientation of service. To elaborate, Moore (1970) substantiated Goode's (1957, 1969) suggestions that members of a profession must allow the welfare of the client to guide their decisions. The orientation of service is a fitting notion applicable to the academy presidency. According to Moore, the orientation of service is comprised of interrelated principles: rules of competence, performance, and loyalty. Moore contended that the orientation to service is a conceptual value that cannot always be assessed effectively. As a result, Moore stated that the rules of competence, performance, and loyalty were subcategories of the service orientation value and that these subcategories could provide an alignment through which orientation of service can be scaled. These concepts reinforce the contextual construct of relational congruency and instigate discussions vis-à-vis their applicability to president–faculty relationships. Each of the eight tenets described here may be subsumed under one of these three principles.

Rules of Competence

Moore's (1970, 14) description of competence stipulates standards for admission into the profession that include an abstract body of knowledge but "also maintenance and improvement of both individual and collective standards." An understanding of the formal and informal policies that regulate colleges and universities is a critical component in the rules of competence. Practical and functional knowledge of institutional policies, state and federal law, and accreditation association rules are key aspects to presidential and institutional success. Moore concluded that lack of competence results in harm to the client.

Tenets One and Seven fit within the parameters of Moore's competence element. A president's knowledge and understanding of the formal and informal rules are vital to his or her ability to provide service.

Rules of Performance

Due to their position at the apex of the academy hierarchy, college and university presidents not only represent the ethos of the institution (Romesburg 2010) but also the well-being of the various constituencies that support the institution. The general rule of performance predicates that the president is obligated to act in the welfare of the institution's constituencies (Moore 1970). The lack of knowledge that constituencies have concerning the various nuances of the president's role is also acknowledged in the rule of performance (Davis and Davis 1999; Miller and Pope 2003). Tenets Two, Three, and Five pertain to this particular rule.

Rules of Loyalty

The development and cultivation of relationships extends from the mutual trust and good will that is shared between the various parties. Moore's (1970) rules of loyalty reinforce the idea that the welfare of the client is paramount. Faculty, staff, students, the community, and other institutional constituency groups entrust academy presidents to champion the traditions, values, and the mission of the institution. Deviation from this path constitutes an infringement on the rules of loyalty. This rule also addresses the decision-making process of institutional presidents and behavior missteps that hinder the well-being of the client. The development of coalitions and the engagement of stakeholders in advancing the mission of the institution and achieving its goals is a fundamental aspect of this particular rule. Tenets Four, Six, and Eight contribute to the president's ability to establish trust, cultivate relationships, and thus promulgate loyalty.

Inaugurating a Presidential Code of Conduct

The acquisition of presidential legitimacy in the academic community is gained through the development of trust and the perception of "cultural fit"

NEW DIRECTIONS FOR HIGHER EDUCATION • DOI:10.1002/he

among the constituencies of the institution. Institutional stakeholders confer legitimacy on presidents who reflect the institution's culture and demonstrate behaviors and values that represent the preeminent interests and social norms of the institution's stakeholders. An inherent obstacle in presidential leadership originates from the various and numerous constituency clusters with which a president must interact. Each group conceptualizes the role of the president differently and demonstrates variant perceptions of the institutional mission and values.

The development and implementation of a presidential code of conduct dictate change in the institutional coalitions, presidential evaluation process, and professional training stages. Consistency of institutional message, mission, values, and expectations is the foundations of this imperative change. The following recommendations simplify the tumultuous nature of developing relational congruency, support the welfare of the institution and its constituencies, and provide transparency of expectations for the role performance of academy presidents.

1. Academy stakeholders must strive to develop corporate priorities and expectations. The complexity of colleges and universities has stimulated and increased institutional fragmentation. To validate a presidential code of conduct, continuity of institutional mission, values, and expectations is paramount. The fluid expectations of political participants and social engagers within the academic milieu must explore and develop common institutional missions and goals supported by cooperative values. The development of cooperative values clarifies the ambiguous nature of presidential boundaries and compartmentalizes the role of the president as the chief administrative officer.

2. Assessment of the president's performance should incorporate involvement from the various institutional constituencies; however, the evaluation of the president should focus on the corporate institutional priorities and values. Presidential assessments should examine the president's progress toward satisfying institutional goals (Fisher 1996). This recommendation supports the corporate values and the construct of inclusion and engagement proposed by the eight tenets. It provides academy presidents with clear understanding of expectations and the measures by which they will be evaluated.

   The relational congruency of the faculty and the board provides an essential prerequisite to this recommendation. According to a 2009 report by the Association of Governing Boards of Universities and Colleges, the mutual engagement of board members, presidents, and institutional faculty provides fertile ground for a healthy academy. Faculty collaboration and participation on board committees are important elements to engaging the full spectrum of the shared governance apparatus. Substantive engagement in board–faculty relationships cultivates congruency as trustees and faculty develop a stronger understanding of their respective governance roles. This report states that faculty has the authority to influence policy change and should be afforded the opportunity to engage boards on key matters such as presidential assessment. Faculty leadership occupies a strategic position to observe many of the day-to-day presidential behaviors and decisions because faculty have the opportunity to interact with the president on matters concerning the campus. Conversely, many boards are separated from their institutions by time, space, and competing demands. "Although some board members on some campuses like to insinuate themselves into the daily activities of a campus, the role of most boards is relatively contained" (Tierney 2005, 6) and relegated to fiduciary issues and maintaining the political solvency of the institution. Numerous constituent groups maintain a vested interest in the success of their institution. Lachs (2011, 5) states that some of these groups including faculty, staff, and students occupy a close internal perspective on the role performance of the president whereas external groups such as trustees are unable to assess the role performance of the president due to their distance and lack of qualifications to "question the managers they have hired."

The education and training of current and future academy presidents must be addressed as well. Presidents should understand their professional boundaries, their role, and the standards by which their performance and leadership are being assessed.

3. One of the challenges of the academy presidency is that there is no formal training that prepares a candidate to meet its challenges. Accordingly, colleges and universities should look to provide continuous professional development opportunities for the president. Training programs that afford presidents opportunities to gain formal training and knowledge on managerial, leadership, and fiduciary topics are advantageous to the success of the president and the welfare of the institution. In addition, these professional development opportunities provide presidents the occasion to dialogue with other presidents by providing networking opportunities and access to resources that otherwise would go unrealized. The education and continuous development of academy presidents is a missing piece of today's leadership matrix. The tenets of the presidential code of ethics should be used to provide training and understanding concerning the role of the president, the academy as an evolving organization, and the various roles and association that affect and are affected by the institution.

It is realistic to acknowledge that some may not understand or give credence to the development of a presidential code of conduct. The intrinsic nature of the academy presidency involves a broad scope of responsibilities, complexity of duties, and an ambiguity of the rules. Understanding the presidency from every aspect or constituent perspective is impossible, too fluid, and unneeded. Unlike other academy stakeholders involved in the success of the institution, academy faculty members are strategically positioned to assist the president in charting and maintaining the cultural values and academic continuity of the institution (Davis and Davis 1999). It is the faculty who shapes the image of a new president (Bensimon 1991), bestows presidential legitimacy (Bornstein 2003), and adjudicates the values and behavior personified by the president (Fleming 2010). Unlike other internal constituencies, faculties hold a central position to engage the academy's administration and influence the president.

Conclusion

A presidential code of conduct is needed more today than ever before. College and university presidents are being required to do more without the proper training to succeed. Presidents from outside the academy enter academia with normative patterns and codes of conduct that served them well in their previous occupations but now have the potential to be detrimental within the collegiate environment. The development of a presidential code of conduct supports the growth and success of the institution, encourages relationship congruency, and strengthens the cooperative partnerships between the president and the institutional faculty.

The evolution of the college and university presidency is not complete. The professoriate may not ever understand the full scope of the presidential office or the individual who occupies the office. Nevertheless, understanding the role each member plays in the relationship and the boundaries that govern the interactions of the relationship enables the participating partners to step in the "right" direction at the same time.

References

American Council on Education. 2012. *The American College President.* Washington, DC: American Council on Education.

Association of Governing Boards of Universities and Colleges. 2009. *Faculty, Governing Boards, and Institutional Governance.* Accessed June 8, 2012. http://agb.org/sites/agb.org/files/u16/FacultyGoverning%20BoardsandInstitutionalGovernance_final.pdf.

Balderston, F. E. 1995. *Managing Today's University.* San Francisco: Jossey-Bass.

Bensimon, E. M. 1991. "The Social Processes through which Faculty Shape the Image of a New President." *Journal of Higher Education* 62(6): 637–660.

Birnbaum, R. 1988. *How Colleges Work.* San Francisco: Jossey-Bass.

Birnbaum, R. 1989. "Responsibility Without Authority: The Impossible Job of the College President." In *Higher Education: Handbook of Theory and Research.* Vol. 5, edited by J. C. Smart. New York: Agathon Press.

Birnbaum, R. 1992. *How Academic Leadership Works: Understanding Success and Failure in the College Presidency.* San Francisco: Jossey-Bass.

Birnbaum, R. 2002. "The President as Storyteller: Restoring the Narrative of Higher Education." *The Presidency* 5(3): 32–39.

Bolman, L. G., and T. E. Deal. 1997. *Reframing Organizations: Artistry, Choice, and Leadership,* 2nd ed. San Francisco: Jossey-Bass.

Bornstein, R. 2003. *Legitimacy in the Academic Presidency: From Entrance to Exit*. Westport, CT: Praeger.

Boschken, H. L. 1994. "Organizational Performance and Multiple Constituencies." *Administrative Review* 54(3): 308–312.

Braxton, J. M. 2010. "Norms and the Work of Colleges and Universities: Introduction to the Special Issue—Norms in Academia." *Journal of Higher Education* 81(3): 243–250.

Bray, N. J. 2003. "Faculty Perceptions of Academic Deans: Stakeholders, Boundary-Spanning, and Social Control." PhD diss., Vanderbilt University.

Cohen, M. D., and J. G. March. 1974. *Leadership and Ambiguity*, 2nd ed. Boston: Harvard Business School Press.

Davis, W. E., and D. R. Davis. 1999. "The University Presidency: Do Evaluations Make a Difference?" *Journal of Personnel Evaluation in Education* 13(2): 119–140.

Dennison, G. M. 2001. "Small Men on Campus: Modern University Presidents." *Innovative Higher Education* 25(4): 269–284.

Fain, P. 2006. "Crisis of Confidence." *Chronicle of Higher Education* 52(42): A28.

Fain, P. 2008. "Photo Finishes a Presidency, and Illustrates a New Risk." *Chronicle of Higher Education*, August 29. http://chronicle.com/article/Photo-Finishes-a-Presidency/ 1114/.

Fisher, J. L. 1996. "Taking a Closer Look at Presidential Reviews." *Educational Record* 77(2–3): 56–60.

Fleming, J. C. 2010. "Faculty Expectations for College Presidents." *Journal of Higher Education* 81(3): 251–283.

Goode, W. J. 1957. "Community within a Community: The Professions." *American Sociological Review* 22(2): 194–200.

Goode, W. J. 1969. "The Theoretical Limits of Professionalization." In *The Semi-Professions and Their Organizations*, edited by A. Etzioni. New York: Free Press.

Guess, A. 2007. "President Fired after Drunk Driving Charges." *Inside Higher Ed*, May 1. http://www.insidehighered.com/print/news/2007/05/01/frawley?width=775& height=500&frame=true.

Hebel, S. 2012. "U. of Illinois President Resigns in Wake of Widespread Faculty Criticism." *Chronicle of Higher Education*, March 22. http://chronicle.com/ article/U-of-Illinois-President/131284/.

Johnston, S. W. 2003. "Faculty Governance and Effective Academic Administrative Leadership." In *Identifying and Preparing Academic Leaders,* New Directions for Higher Education, no. 124, 57–63, edited by S. L. Hoppe and B. W. Speck. San Francisco: Jossey-Bass.

Koch, J. V., and J. L. Fisher. 1996. *Presidential Leadership: Making a Difference*. Phoenix: Oryx Press.

Lachs, J. 2011. "Shared Governance Is a Myth." *Chronicle of Higher Education* 57(23): A64.

Lester, J. 2010. "Malone University President Steps Down amid Plagiarism Accusations." *Chronicle of Higher Education*, February 22. http://chronicle.com/article/ malone-U-President-Steps-Down/64328/.

Masterson, K. 2009. "U. of Illinois President Resigns in Wake of Admissions Scandal." *Chronicle of Higher Education*, September 23. http://chronicle.com/ article/U-of-Illinois-President/48587/.

McGill, A., M. Assad, and D. P. Sheehan. 2011. "Penn State President Graham Spanier Resigns in Wake of Scandal." *Morning Call*, November 10. http://articles.mcall. com/2011–11–10/sports/mc-penn-state-spanier-20111109_1_joe-paterno -president-graham-spanier-penn-state.

McGoey, S. P. 2007. "A Comparison of Institutional Stakeholder's Perceptions of Presidential Effectiveness." *International Journal of Educational Management* 21(2): 86–104.

Michael, S. O., M. Schwartz, and L. Balraj. 2001. "Indicators of Presidential Effective-ness: A Study of Trustees of Higher Education Institutions." *International Journal of Education Management* 15(7): 332–346.

Miller, M. T., and M. L. Pope. 2003. "Faculty Senate Leadership as a Presidential Path-way: Clear Passage or Caught in a Maze?" *Community College Journal of Research and Practice* 27: 119–129.

Moore, W. E. 1970. *The Professions: Roles and Rules.* New York: Russell Sage Foundation.

Neumann, A., and E. M. Bensimon. 1990. "Constructing the Presidency: College Presi-dents' Images of Their Leadership Roles, a Comparative Study." *Journal of Higher Education* 61(6): 687–701.

Olscamp, P. J. 2003. *Moral Leadership: Ethics and the College Presidency.* Lanham, MD: Rowman & Littlefield.

Prator, R. 1963. *The College President.* Washington, DC: Center for Applied Research in Education.

Rogers, B., and M. Tresaugue. 2008. "TSU's Slade Avoids Prison with Plea Deal." *Houston Chronicle,* March 27. http://www.chron.com/news/houston-texas/article/TSU-s-Slade -avoids-prison-with-plea-deal-1584929.php.

Romesburg, K. D. 2010. "Ethical Dimensions of Presidential Leadership." In *The Ethical Challenges of Academic Administration,* edited by E. E. Englehardt, M. S. Pritchard, K. D. Romesburg, and B. E. Schrag. New York: Springer.

Stripling, J. 2012. "U. of Maryland University College President to Resign, But the Rea-son Remains Unexplained." *Chronicle of Higher Education,* March 22. http://chronicle .com/article/U-of-Maryland-University/131281/.

Tierney, W. G. 2005. "When Divorce Is Not an Option: The Board and the Faculty." *Academe* 91(3): 43–46.

Van Der Werf, M. 1999. "A Scandal and a Suicide Leave a College Reeling." *Chronicle of Higher Education,* November 19. http://chronicle.com/article/ A-Scandala-Suicide-Leave/18281.

Walker, D. E. 1981. "The President as Ethical Leader of the Campus." In *Professional Ethics in University Administration,* New Directions for Higher Education, no. 33, 15–27, edited by R. H. Stein and M. C. Baca. San Francisco: Jossey-Bass.

Ward, D. 2002. "The Modern President—Priest, Warrior, or Both?" *The Presidency* 5(3): 9–10.

Welte, M. S. 2003. "President's Arrest Embarrasses College." Seattle Times, March 21. http://community.seattletimes.nwsource.com/archive/?date=20030321&slug=potp rez21.

Wettersten, K. B., and J. W. Lichtenberg. 1995. "Relationship Formation and Change in Psychotherapy: An Analysis of Cases." Paper presented at the Annual Meeting of the American Psychological Association, New York.

J. CHRISTOPHER FLEMING *is the executive director of admissions at Old Dominion University.*

3

This chapter delineates six tenets for a code of conduct to guide the behavior of academic deans.

Follow the Code: Rules or Guidelines for Academic Deans' Behavior?

Nathaniel J. Bray

In the popular movie series *Pirates of the Caribbean*, there is a pirate code that influences how pirates behave in unclear situations, with a running joke about whether the code is either a set of rules or guidelines for behavior. Codes of conduct in any social group or organization can have much the same feel; they can provide clarity and direction but with the question about which elements are rules and which are guidelines. Thus, there is a difference between social mores (more centrally held norms whose violations elicit a strong response), folkways (less centrally held norms whose violations engender a weaker response) (Macionis 2001), and formal rules. All are part of the formation of accepted norms for behavior. However, not all rules are followed perfectly nor are they necessarily expected to be. A classic sociological example is the posted speed limit for automobiles. It may be a formal rule, but many treat it as a guideline, driving at or above the posted maximum but not under its limit. In other areas of life and work, expectations may never be written down, but trouble awaits anyone who violates the unwritten rules.

The point of these examples is that such codes and norms exist across all human organizations. The central task is to find out the status of rules and norms within one's profession, institution, and position. This is especially true for positions in organizations that have multiple stakeholder groups whose perceptions can influence the effectiveness and role set of the given position. Higher education, with its bevy of stakeholder groups, is such an enterprise; almost all of these groups interact with academic deans and can help, constrain, and shape their behavior (Ryan 1980). Given the confusions that can arise, this chapter is devoted to detailing an empirically driven code of conduct for academic deans. Several higher education experts (Austin and Gamson 1983; Birnbaum 1988; Del Favero and Bray

NEW DIRECTIONS FOR HIGHER EDUCATION, no. 160, Winter 2012 © Wiley Periodicals, Inc.
Published online in Wiley Online Library (wileyonlinelibrary.com) • DOI:10.1002/he.20033

2010; Dill 1984; Walker 1981) have hypothesized that there exists within colleges and universities an administrative culture that is different from and often at odds with the faculty academic culture. The suggested logical end for this bifurcated culture is a sense of disconnection or even distrust between faculty and academic administrators (Birnbaum 1988; Dill 1984; Kezar and Eckel 2004), particularly deans who have to work closely with both administrative and faculty stakeholders (Ryan 1980). Several reasons for this disconnection have been posited; for example, one is that over time, deans begin to work more and more with other administrators. As a result, faculty come to associate administrators with an institutional bureaucracy that is increasingly removed from central academic concerns (Birnbaum 1988). Walker (1981) has suggested that over time academic administrators tend to shift toward a shared administrative perspective, or at least they are perceived to do so. This may lead to benefits in shared administrative values and streamlined functioning, but at the same time may well produce declining effectiveness of academic administrators in working with faculty.

Part of the reason for this distrust or sense that administrators and faculty are inherently different may also be due in part to the ambiguity of roles for academic administrators and the number of stakeholders concerned. Academic administrators have complex, yet ambiguous, roles (Wolverton, Wolverton, and Gmelch 2000), working in environments that involve multiple stakeholder groups—from faculty and students to alumni and boards of trustees—that are attempting to move the institution and its principals in various directions (Association of Governing Boards of Universities and Colleges 1996; Cohen and March 1974; Montez, Wolverton, and Gmelch 2003; Wolverton, Wolverton, and Gmelch 2000). Because academic deans not only have to perform their roles effectively but also ascertain what their role should be in the given context, the challenge facing them is intensified. A wrong choice on the appropriate role set can lead to a perception of being ineffective, regardless of how effective individual decisions are. Faculty perceptions of administrators' effectiveness in particular are important to administrative success (Bensimon 1991).

The distrust and faculty concern about administrators overstepping their bounds comes despite the fact that many academic administrators and those in levels of upper administration come from the same experiential backgrounds as faculty members (Blackburn and Lawrence 1995; Cohen and March 1974). As a result, the impact of the perceived distance between deans and faculty may be exacerbated by a general inability of the faculty to fathom the move to the deanship, in which the former faculty members frequently relinquish much of their teaching and research time. Faculty view such movement as deans changing or leaving the academic profession (Goode 1969) as problematic and, it would seem, difficult to understand. Movement through tenure and promotion to full professor and then ultimately to dean involves such a laborious and extended socialization process in values and thinking that is, in a sense, nonadministrative, that many faculty find it difficult to fathom the inner workings of someone who would make that choice. Also, there has been a long trend of bureaucratic accretion (Gumport and Pusser 1995), that is, more administrative positions as compared to the respective number of faculty positions at some institutions. This adds another possible area for faculty distrust. There may be a sense on the part of faculty that as a professionalized administrative culture grows, adding more administrators reduces the number of faculty positions (Del Favero and Bray 2010).

One key place to look for the possible growth and impact of an administrative culture would be at the deans' level, which Ryan (1980) suggests is a linchpin position in the middle of a hierarchical administrative culture and a horizontal faculty culture. As a result of their central position within college and university systems, deans fulfill what is often called a boundary-spanning role (Manev and Stevenson 2001) in which they seek to interact with all constituencies and to assess the insights and needs of each constituency. The success of their work involves perhaps most centrally their ability to effectively work with faculty and administrators both, as they serve at the intersection of the horizontal and vertical cultures of the institution (Ryan 1980).

Those administrators who do survive and fit with the administrative cultural norms may over time be viewed as having less and less in common with the faculty (Austin and Gamson 1983), particularly if they stay in the position for more than a three- to six-year period. In fact, staying in the administrative ranks, particularly at the higher levels, is seen as removing oneself from the faculty position; the higher the individual moves up the administrative hierarchy, the more removed and distant the faculty members generally feel from the administrator in question (Dill 1984). Thus, deans are deemed by many to have, and may indeed feel, a set of perspectives and values more similar to those administrators they report to (provosts and presidents) than to the faculty.

Del Favero and Bray (2010) in a review of the faculty–administrator relationship point to areas in teaching, research, hiring and contracts, and promotion and tenure, among others that can lead to differences in opinion and tensions between these two stakeholder groups. The basis of this study draws upon many of the postulated tensions that can exist in the dean's role, as these tensions have an impact on the dean's administrative duties and on working effectively with faculty in these areas (Bray 2008, 2010; Del Favero and Bray 2010).

Why should we care about how the role of the dean is viewed by various stakeholders? Bensimon (1991), Neumann (1995), and Fincher (1996) have all illustrated that the way in which others understand and view the work of the administrator plays a large role in defining and either supporting or limiting the administrator's future success. Deans therefore are heavily regulated by social norms and expectations (Bray 2008; Cohen and

March 1974; Ryan 1980). Unfortunately, differing expectations that faculty and administrators have of deans can be confusing, as Kezar and Eckel (2004) note. This can lead to decreased morale and increased conflict; it is often difficult to strike an open and cooperative balance between the two groups (Welsh and Metcalf 2003). In fact, Bray (2008) has shown that different individual faculty members and faculty groups can hold disparate expectations for deans' normative behavior. However, as posited here, it is not just the flat and often low-consensus faculty culture that is a challenge. Bray (2003), for instance, showed that male and female faculty had profoundly different perspectives on the appropriateness of deans' behavior.

The enforcement of norms also may differ based on one's position within the profession. Thus, senior faculty may hold a different and possibly stricter sense of what types of behavior are inappropriate for academic deans. Race and gender may also play a factor in perspectives of institutional and administrative functioning. The type, mission, and nature of the institution also may influence how stakeholders perceive administrative behavior (Birnbaum 1988). This chapter seeks to draw across all these categories to develop widely applicable tenets.

Differing external bodies of which academic deans might be members offer some suggestions for behavior. The American Association of University Administrators (AAUA) (1994) offers a list of eighteen behaviors that should guide administrative action. Standards listed include dyadic statements of rights and responsibilities on such topical areas as nondiscrimination, expression of personal opinions, and fair and equitable treatment. The responsibilities listed in the AAUA guide come the closest to being tenets or codes of conduct in articulating the obligation of administrators to make sure a proper environment exists on campus in these several areas. However, these standards are not specifically targeted to academic deans and do not deal in depth with their particular decision and role areas.

Individual institutions also have codes for internal stakeholder behavior. Edmondson (1992) conducted a review of 100 sets of institutional codes of ethics for the largest two-year colleges in each U.S. state. Another 68 two-year institutions said they had no such code. Of the 100 codes submitted in his review, only 5 were for the administrator (nonpresident) level. In another study Rifkin (1993) found that of 413 responding community colleges, only 36 had a form of administrator ethics policy. From these, she found four main policy categories: conflict of interest, nepotism, integrity, and accountability.

Deans may also benefit from learning about norms or unofficial codes of conduct from other deans, either through written communication (often in the forms of books about how to be a dean) or through professional conferences and institutes. For example, in 2012, the American Conference of Academic Deans (ACAD) held an institute for deans to network and learn from each other. The American Association of Community Colleges (AACC) also has a recommended code of ethics (2005) that pertains to and affects those individuals who fill dean-like positions in community colleges. The scattered nature of these efforts and lack of a consistently and empirically crafted code of conduct for deans give rise to the effort of this chapter.

Norms for Academic Deans

What do we know about norms for academic deans specifically? Still relatively little. In an empirical study of faculty perceptions of academic deans' behavior, Bray (2008) found eleven norms across three levels for academic deans' behavior. The original study drew 205 faculty nationwide using a stratified, random cluster sampling from across four disciplines (biology, chemistry, history, and sociology) and two institutional types (liberal arts and research institutions, using the Carnegie 2000 typology).

In 2010, Bray further developed the topic to consider connections between faculty perceptions and Mertonian (Merton 1973) norms for science (universalism, communality, disinterestedness, and organized skepticism) to examine whether the norms of science translated to administration. The 2010 work found only moderate support for the Mertonian norms as translated into administrative behavior and instead proffered four key broad norms for administrative behavior that serve as an additional framework for the tenets and code of conduct proposed here for academic deans. These eleven groupings from the 2008 work and four groupings from the 2010 work are highlighted next in the appropriate area with the tenets they support.

Code of Conduct for Academic Deans

Any code of conduct must remain flexible and somewhat vague to allow for the variances due to context. Although the general principles behind the tenets listed here are supported across institutional types and disciplines, there is always a question of scale (how much of the given behavior is acceptable before there is a response) and of context (how much of institutional history, for example, changes the way these tenets should be applied). For example, in an institution that has removed a dean for fiscal impropriety, the next dean will likely be under tighter scrutiny and should consider even more carefully the tenets related to fiduciary responsibilities.

With that in mind, the following tenets are offered to guide academic deans' behavior. In developing the tenets, the following criteria were applied: (1) they should be supported by empirical evidence rather than being opinion-driven lists of subsidized or proscribed behaviors, and (2) they should apply to each of the major groups and areas with which academic deans work. As noted, they draw on Bray's (2008; 2010) work on norms for academic deans.

Academic Deans Should Be Outstanding Communicators. They should establish and maintain open, honest, and timely chains of communication. There is a balance between too much and too little information, a fine line that faculty members expect deans to try to walk. There is the added challenge of trying to communicate in the style and at the level of data expected for the hierarchical culture of administration, the flat faculty culture, as well as the culture of staff and nonacademic administrators. As noted in Bray (2010), almost half of the norms in Bray (2008) deal with communication of one kind or another. Thus, this tenet fits with Bray's (2008) norms of *Inept Evaluation and Representation*, which includes items on support documentation for promotion and tenure; *Failure to Communicate*, which includes items on faculty input; and *Undermining Faculty Control*, which includes items about not seeking input from faculty or letting them know of items such as budgetary issues. *Disdain for Faculty Input* also was informative here. This norm includes items about not informing faculty of decisions in which faculty are expected to provide input. Under the norm, *Unconveyed Expectations*, deans are expected to be able to clearly communicate faculty views. However, it is important to note that deans have some leeway here, as faculty members seem to accept that deans sometime need to withhold information for strategic reasons.

Academic Deans Should Be Transparent. They should provide clear expectations, and be a clarifying force, for faculty and staff success.

Deans should be a voice of clarity and reliability in promotion and tenure processes. One of the challenges in higher education, given the noted role ambiguity and vagaries of promotion and tenure, is the ability to gauge one's own progress and plot avenues to success. To help address this challenge, the dean needs to develop a clear set of roles and responsibilities within his or her office and help faculty develop and promulgate expectations for faculty success in the tenure and promotion process. Bray's (2008) norm of *Unconveyed Expectations* provides an argument for suggesting this norm as it includes items such as not providing expectations for success, for teaching, or for the specific roles of nonacademic administrators.

Academic Deans Should Be Colleagues. They should strive to seek and follow faculty input on programmatic and curricular decisions.

Deans should follow agreed upon decisions, particularly in programmatic, curricular, and budgetary decisions. Although deans have a critical role in decision making, governance models often discuss the importance of faculty, and faculty disposition to be in control of, programmatic and curricular issues. However, efforts need to be made to take care of both important stakeholders' legitimate concerns. This fits with Bray's (2008) norms of *Undermining Faculty Control*, which includes items about ignoring or not seeking faculty input; *Failure to Communicate*, which includes items such as "Does not seek faculty input in making programmatic decisions"; and *Disdain for Faculty Input*, which includes items such as failing to follow through on faculty input for departmental direction.

Academic Deans Should Be Judges. They should establish and oversee a culture of morality and justice on campus.

New Directions for Higher Education • DOI:10.1002/he

Deans should pursue instances of wrongdoing in an exemplary fashion. As the visible head and representative of a college, deans need to know that they represent the college at all times. Although it is important for them to note when they are expressing their own opinions, their behavior in making those opinions known will also affect public opinion about their respective colleges. Thus, they should make decisions as if they are always being watched and present themselves appropriately. The related behaviors, as found by Bray (2008) include *Failure to Communicate,* which includes items such as not discussing students complaints without faculty before moving forward; *Regulatory Disdain,* which includes items such as violating rules and regulations or becoming involved romantically with students; and *Inept Evaluation and Representation,* which includes items such as not giving due process in promotion and tenure decisions. Deans are also expected to stand firm in their values and not put the institution at risk by violating rules or regulations (see Bray's [2008] norm of *Bending to Pressure*).

Academic Deans Should Be Exemplars of Professional Tone and Behavior. This aligns with Bray's (2008) norms of *Being Publicly Critical,* which includes items related to criticizing faculty and staff in front of others; and *Devaluing Nonacademic Staff,* which includes items such as failing to acknowledge the accomplishments of others or taking credit for other people's ideas. Deans should follow classic organizational and leadership behaviors of supporting others, celebrating success, and being open to different opinions.

Academic Deans Should Be Sound Fiscal Managers. Bray's (2008) norm of *Fiscal Intemperance* speaks directly to this concept, in which faculty show strong displeasure to deans who take funds earmarked for use in one area and then use them elsewhere, when deans do not follow a formal budget, and when they spend without prioritization.

Where to Go from Here?

Empirically based tenets for a code of conduct can be helpful for deans beginning to learn the expectations for their new position. Given that their prior work is generally in the faculty realm and that professional development institutes for deans are still relatively few and limited in scope, a focused code of ethics has potential to be a powerful tool. Yahr, Bryan, and Schimmel (2009) make several excellent points about building useful codes. They state that codes must be audited for usefulness and reviewed periodically to remind stakeholders that they exist and what is valued. Codes of ethics are likely to have more traction if stakeholders are engaged in helping make the codes. That is why this research sought empirical information from across various institutional types and stakeholder types. Although the tenets may be held more or less strongly at various specific settings, they are based on empirical views across stakeholders groups about how the position of the academic deanship is viewed and how the person in that role should behave.

Following the postulations of Yahr et al. (2009), it is possible to make several recommendations for how a code of conduct should be used to help prepare deans.

1. *Necessitate.* Policy-makers and upper-level administrators should assert that an administrator code of conduct is necessary. Along with providing role and goal clarity, this code would create valuable expectations for *how* work should be done on campus without unduly constraining *what* should be done.

2. *Contextualize.* Although the tenets that underpin codes of conduct have been drawn from across stakeholder groups and institutional types with the desire to make such codes as universal as possible for academic deans, the reality is that institutions can vary a great deal in some key ways, even when structures look nearly identical. The new dean should seek to find information about and from key stakeholder groups that help provide the context and background to go with these overarching areas.

3. *Evaluate.* Behavior needs to be checked against normative expectations. Doing so in a regular, formative manner allows for growth and refinement (that is, helps contextualize) before behaviors depart from the norms and strong sanction or change becomes necessary.

4. *Disseminate.* Tenets of a code and expectations for the field will increasingly help the more ingrained the field becomes. Expectations in professional associations and in training as mentioned at the beginning of this chapter will help build a critical conversation and shared set of goals and expectations. Inclusion of codes into the accreditation process would formalize the points made here. There are several avenues to pursue. Disciplinary associations should note specific expectations for administrator behavior. These efforts should be targeted specifically at the chair and dean levels given the focus on disciplinary specific concerns. For institutional accreditation through regional accrediting organizations, specific expectations should be stated for specific administrative positions, including the academic dean. Not only would this help reduce role ambiguity, it would help anchor core values for how to perform the roles associated with the deanship.

Conclusion

The deanship is a critically difficult position. At a presentation the author made at a recent meeting of the Association for the Study of Higher Education on the difficulties of the deanship and its inherent role ambiguities, one of the audience members called out, "Why does anyone do it?!" To many faculty who value what they do on a day-to-day basis, this question makes a lot of sense. And yet, given the centrality of the deanship and the growth of accountability and bureaucratic accretion, the position is becoming more and more important. It is critical that we seek the best information we can to make the transition to, and fulfilling of, that position as deliberate as we can. A code of conduct can help not only academic deans; it can also help other stakeholders understand how the collective entity of higher education views what deans do and how they should do it.

References

American Association of Community Colleges. 2005. *Recommended Code of Ethics for CEOs of Community Colleges.* http://www.aacc.nche.edu/About/Positions/Pages/ps11102005.aspx.

American Association of University Administrators (AAUA). 1994. *A.A.U.A. Statement of Professional Standards for Administrators in Higher Education.* http://www.aaua.org/aboutus/aboutus.htm.

Association of Governing Boards of Universities and Colleges. 1996. *Renewing the Academic Presidency: Stronger Leadership for Tougher Times.* Washington, DC: AGBUC.

Austin, A. E., and Z. F. Gamson. 1983. *Academic Workplace: New Demands, Heightened Tensions.* ASHE-ERIC Higher Education Research Report no. 10. Washington, DC: Association for the Study of Higher Education.

Bensimon, E. M. 1991. "The Social Processes through which Faculty Shape the Image of a New President." *Journal of Higher Education* 62(6): 637–660.

Birnbaum, R. 1988. *How Colleges Work: The Cybernetics of Academic Organization and Leadership.* San Francisco: Jossey-Bass.

Blackburn, R. T., and J. H. Lawrence. 1995. *Faculty at Work.* Baltimore: Johns Hopkins University Press.

Bray, N. J. 2003. "Faculty Perceptions of Academic Deans: Stakeholders, Boundary-Spanning, and Social Control." PhD diss., Vanderbilt University.

Bray, N. J. 2008. "Proscriptive Norms for Academic Deans: Comparing Faculty Expectations across Institutional and Disciplinary Boundaries." *Journal of Higher Education* 79(6): 692–721.

Bray, N. J. 2010. "The Deanship and Its Faculty Interpreters: Do Mertonian Norms of Science Translate into Norms for Administration?" *Journal of Higher Education* 81(3): 284–316.

Cohen, M. D., and J. G. March. 1974. *Leadership and Ambiguity: The American College President.* New York: McGraw-Hill.

Del Favero, M., and N. J. Bray. 2010. "Herding Cats and Big Dogs: Tensions in the Faculty-Administrator Relationship." In *Higher Education: Handbook of Theory and Research,* no. 25: 477–541. New York: Springer.

Dill, D. D. 1984. "The Nature of Administrative Behavior in Higher Education." *Educational Administration Quarterly* 20(3): 69–99.

Edmondson, W. F. 1992. *A Content Analysis of Codes of Ethics and Related Documents from 100 of America's Largest Community, Junior, and Technical Colleges.* Fulton, MS: Itawamba Community College. (ERIC Document Reproduction Service No. ED 342 451).

Fincher, C. 1996. "Theory and Research in Administrative Leadership." In *Higher Education: Handbook of Theory and Research,* Vol. 11, edited by J. C. Smart. New York: Agathon.

Goode, W. J. 1969. "The theoretical limits of professionalization." In *The Semi-Professions and Their Organizations,* edited by A. Etzioni. New York: Free Press.

Gumport, P., and B. Pusser. 1995. "A Case of Bureaucratic Accretion: Context and Consequences." *Journal of Higher Education* 66(5): 493–520.

Kezar, A., and P. D. Eckel. 2004. "Meeting Today's Governance Challenges: A Synthesis of the Literature and Examination of a Future Agenda for Scholarship." *Journal of Higher Education* 75: 371–399.

Macionis, J. J. 2001. *Sociology,* 8th ed. Upper Saddle River, NJ: Prentice Hall.

Manev, I. M., and W. B. Stevenson, 2001. "Balancing Ties: Boundary Spanning and Influence in the Organization's Extended Network of Communication." *Journal of Business Communication* 38(2): 183–205.

Merton, R. K. 1973. *The Sociology of Science: Theoretical and Empirical Investigations.* Chicago: University of Chicago Press.

Montez, J. M., M. Wolverton, and W. H. Gmelch. 2003. "The Roles and Challenges of Deans." *Review of Higher Education* 26: 241–266.

Neumann, A. 1995. "On the Making of Hard Times and Good Times: The Social Construction of Resource Stress." *Journal of Higher Education* 66: 3–31.

Rifkin, T. 1993. *Administrator and Faculty Ethics Codes in Community Colleges.* ERIC Digest. Los Angeles, CA: ERIC Clearinghouse for Community Colleges. (ERIC Document Reproduction Service No. ED 360 037).

Ryan, D. 1980. "Deans as Individuals-in-Organizations." In *The Dilemma of the Deanship,* edited by D. E. Griffths and D. J. McCarty. Danville, IL: Interstate Publishers and Printers.

Walker, D. E. 1981. "The President as Ethical Leader of the Campus." In *Professional Ethics in University Administration.* New Directions for Higher Education, no. 33, edited by R. H. Stein and M. C. Baca, 15–27. San Francisco: Jossey-Bass.

Welsh, J. F., and J. Metcalf. 2003. "Faculty and Administrative Support for Institutional Effectiveness Activities: A Bridge Across the Chasm." *Journal of Higher Education* 74: 445–468.

Wolverton, M., M. L. Wolverton, and W. H. Gmelch. 2000. "The Impact of Role Conflict and Ambiguity on Academic Deans." *Journal of Higher Education* 70: 80–106.

Yahr, M. A., L. D. Bryan, and K. Schimmel. 2009. "Perceptions of College and University Codes of Ethics." *Journal of Academic and Business Ethics* 2.

NATHANIEL J. BRAY *is an associate professor and program coordinator in Higher Education Administration at the University of Alabama. His research interests include normative structures for academic administrators, sociology of higher education, and student issues across higher education.*

NEW DIRECTIONS FOR HIGHER EDUCATION • DOI:10.1002/he

4

The work of admissions officers serves clients who include prospective students and their families and the college or university they represent. This chapter presents tenets toward a code of conduct for admissions work that safeguards the welfare of such clients.

A Normative Code of Conduct for Admissions Officers

Robert L. Hodum

The increasing competition for the desired quantity and quality of college students, along with the rise of for-profit institutions, has amplified the scrutiny of behavior and ethics among college admissions professionals and has increased the need for meaningful ethical guidelines and codes of conduct. Many other areas of responsibility within the higher education community have adopted codes of ethics or codes of conduct. Some examples of these areas include:

- The ACHE (Association for Continuing Higher Education) Code of Ethics for administrators working in continuing education
- The NAFSA (National Association of Foreign Student Advisers) Statement of Ethics for those working with international and exchange students
- The NASFAA (National Association of Student Financial Aid Administrators) Statement of Ethical Principles for those working in financial aid offices
- The CASE (Council for Advancement and Support of Education) Statement of Ethics for those with responsibilities in the areas of alumni, development, and marketing
- The ACUHO-I (Association of College and University Housing Officers-International) Standards and Ethical Principles for those working with students in institutional residential facilities
- The NASPA-Student Affairs Administrators in Higher Education Standards of Professional Practice for those working in the student affairs areas

NEW DIRECTIONS FOR HIGHER EDUCATION, no. 160, Winter 2012 © Wiley Periodicals, Inc.
Published online in Wiley Online Library (wileyonlinelibrary.com) • DOI:10.1002/he.20034

The admissions-recruiting profession is certainly no exception. For the admissions officer, professional associations and codes of ethics go hand in hand. Although there are many associations, the flagship organizations are the National Association for College Admission Counseling (NACAC) and the American Association of Collegiate Registrars and Admission Officers (AACRAO). NACAC can trace its roots back to the 1930s when ethical issues with regard to recruiting students and awarding scholarships were topics of intense discussion at its meetings (www.nacacnet.org/about/history). The association has developed its Statement of Principles of Good Practice (SPGP), which includes "practices and policies reflecting principled concerns for the ethical treatment of students and relationships among professionals in the admission process" (www.nacacnet.org/about/Governance/Policies/Documents/SPGP_EMPP.pdf). AACRAO also has a strong commitment to help professionals follow standards of ethical behavior as evidenced by the AACRAO Statement of Professional Ethics and Practice (www.aacrao.org/About-AACRAO/ethics-and-practice.aspx).

These two organizations have clearly delineated their commitment to maintaining a standard of ethical behavior among professionals involved in the recruiting and admission of students; however, each association has taken a different approach. AACRAO's statement reads like a walk through a garden of lofty ideals, with examples such as "AACRAO members shall conduct themselves with integrity, fairness, honesty, and respect for others," and "AACRAO members shall assist students to develop their talents and interests and become responsible citizens." Juxtaposed to these broad guidelines is NACAC's Statement of Principles of Good Practice, which reads more like a code of ethical rules, each inserted to respond to a specific abuse, rather than a broader statement of principles (Jump 1995). Some examples are "Members agree that they will not use disparaging comparisons of secondary or postsecondary institutions" and "Members agree that they will not publicly announce the amount of need-based aid awarded to any student without his/her permission."

The need for such codes of conduct has been obvious, not only from within the admissions profession but also from others in higher education and business communities. In the Carnegie Foundation report, *College*, Ernest Boyer (1987) suggests that institutions should, above all, tell their stories with integrity and good taste. Boyer and other researchers have found that most institutions are ethical in their procedures of recruiting; however, many researchers are also concerned that increased marketing may become the means that drives the end. Evidence of a growing abuse of codes of ethics in the profession goes back over twenty years when Johnson (1989, 27) reported that "commissions are paid, many publications do exaggerate reality, recruitment strategies often coerce, and financial aid awarding is sometimes analogous to poker betting strategies."

Many admissions representatives are asking questions about these codes of conduct and what seems to be a growing resistance to ethical

NEW DIRECTIONS FOR HIGHER EDUCATION • DOI:10.1002/he

behavior in the profession. Are the NACAC and AACRAO statements working to improve the situation? Are there ways to bring about improvements that do not involve these two national organizations? Hodum and James (2010) found that the level of familiarity with NACAC's Statement of Principles of Good Practice (SPGP) does indeed have an effect on the level of disdain admissions officers have for misbehaviors. In other words, as an admissions officer's familiarity with the SPGP increases, they are increasingly offended by the recruiting misbehaviors. These findings stemmed from Hodum's (2007) research known as the National Study of College Admissions and Recruiting Behaviors (NSCARB), in which he administered the College Admission and Recruiting Behaviors Inventory (CARBI). The survey results and the resulting empirical analyses provide the foundation for recommendations and suggestions that follow in this article.

McDonough and Robertson (1995) indicated clear evidence of a growing trend toward professionalization among admissions officers across the country. Hodum and James (2010) also found this growing professionalization still taking place in more recent years. Grifone-Field, Piersol, and Naticchia (1992) suggest that admissions officers have asked for, and should be granted, greater professional responsibilities and opportunities that have a more significant impact on their institutions and the lives of students. But what does this growth toward professionalization mean for postsecondary admissions-recruiting employees? How do they become more professional?

Sociologists suggest that an occupational group's level of professionalization depends on how many characteristics of a profession these occupations possess (Barber 1962; Carr-Saunders and Wilson 1933; Greenwood 1957; Harries-Jenkins 1970; Millerson 1964; Moore 1970). These characteristics include (a) an extensive period of training and socialization, (b) the possession of a systematic body of theory, (c) the formation of professional associations, and (d) the existence of a code of conduct (Braxton and Bayer 1999). The code of conduct or code of ethics goes hand in hand with the expectations of self-regulation and autonomy found among the professions. Any of these characteristics found to be taking place in the admissions profession, including the development and use of a code of ethics, can be an indication of this growing professionalization trend.

Hodum and James (2010) indicate that the normative patterns emerging from the National Study of College Admissions and Recruiting Behaviors correspond to the formal codes of ethics from NACAC and AACRAO; however, in these times of increased skepticism and suspicion regarding the recruitment of postsecondary students, perhaps the empirical research could spawn additional steps that might work to regain trust from students, parents, and the general public. Perhaps thinking "outside the box" of professional organizations could bring about some meaningful improvements that would protect both students and the institutions that seek their enrollment.

NEW DIRECTIONS FOR HIGHER EDUCATION • DOI:10.1002/he

The existing codes of ethics from AACRAO and NACAC are quite possibly seen as a set of rules to follow, a list of exactly what an officer should do or should not do in order to remain in compliance. It is also possible that the focus remains on the rules, rather than the meaning behind why the rules exist. Do admissions officers know why these rules exist, or are they simply focused on prescriptive and proscriptive codes that their supervisors have suggested admissions officers need to know? Is there a way to take the spotlight off the rule and place it on the protection of the student client? Perhaps the creation of a new code of ethics for admissions officers could simplify behaviors to a short list of expected types of conduct that squarely place the student first. But given the fact that these two professional organizations already have codes of conduct that pertain to admissions officers, how could the creation of a new code be helpful? Where could this new code be effective, and how could it work to strengthen the profession?

First, it is no secret that each reauthorization of the federal Higher Education Act continues to work toward stronger regulation of all postsecondary institutions—both proprietary and nonprofit—by explicitly indicating what institutions can and cannot do (Gould 2009). Most, if not all, states in the United States have some form of a centralized higher education commission that oversees (in various ways) all postsecondary education institutions—public and private, nonprofit and proprietary, four-year and two-year, universities and technical colleges. These higher education commission offices have recently become more involved with distance education providers by requiring specific letters of agreement from any institution wanting to "do business" in their state. It is these state offices that could also be very effective with regard to ethical behavior associated with the recruitment and admission of students. Each state's higher education commission could require every institution to agree to a code of conduct regarding the recruitment and admission of students derived from the tenets proposed in this chapter. This is a bold step in a new direction; however, it could also put the "teeth" into a policy that would slow or stop the unethical recruitment and admission activities taking place across the country.

Second, this newly proposed code of conduct could be used by regional accrediting agencies—Southern Association of Colleges and Schools, Western Association of Schools and Colleges, Northwest Accreditation Commission, North Central Association of Colleges and Schools, New England Association of Schools and Colleges, and the Middle States Association of Colleges and Schools. These accrediting bodies work to ensure that institutions meet the standards established by the higher education community that address the needs of society and students. Institutions seeking accreditation or reaccreditation are generally required to show evidence that they are eligible to participate in programs under Title IV of the Higher Education Act. Some examples of this evidence include showing that their recruiting publications and admission policies accurately represent the institutional mission and are clearly available to students. The regional accrediting agencies could incorporate new standards requiring evidence of adherence to an accepted code of conduct for the recruitment and admission of students.

The tenets of the code proposed herein serve as a foundation for higher education commissions and accrediting bodies to develop their own specific codes. In devising the proposed code, three essential elements were followed: (1) each tenet should safeguard the welfare of students as clients; (2) each tenet should place the interests and needs of the student above those of the institution; and (3) each tenet should emanate from empirical research.

Informal norms are guides to appropriate or inappropriate behavior and provide a basis for the development of the tenets of a formal code of conduct (Braxton and Bayer 2004). Hodum (2007) identified a normative structure for admissions officers, and these norms were empirically derived from the perceptions of 342 admissions officers across the country who were members of AACRAO or NACAC or both associations. These respondents were employed at a variety of institutions including public and private, most competitive to noncompetitive, four-year and two-year, and all levels of Carnegie classification. These empirically derived normative patterns provide the foundation for the tenets of the following code of conduct for admissions officers.

A Code of Conduct for Admissions Officers

Following are nine tenets that higher education commissions and regional accreditation agencies should use in developing a code of conduct. These tenets are related to the empirical findings from Hodum's (2007) National Study of College Admissions and Recruiting Behaviors (NSCARB).

1. *Admissions officers should accurately represent their institution—in printed communication, in electronic communication, and in personal conversation.* Given the competitive nature of recruiting the desired quantity and quality of students, many institutions are tempted to stretch the truth in their printed pieces (Johnson 1989). The copy and the pictures used in both printed pieces and the website should present an accurate picture of an institution's programs, culture, and environment. Admissions officers may find themselves caught up in the competition, and it is not uncommon to hear them exaggerating or sometimes downright lying about the qualities of their campus, faculty, student body, and so forth. Officers must be diligent in presenting accurate information about the institution when they are speaking to prospective students, parents, guidance counselors, and others. This principle was derived from the normative pattern of *institutional misrepresentation*. The proscriptive behaviors indicated

NEW DIRECTIONS FOR HIGHER EDUCATION • DOI:10.1002/he

in this tenet include inadequate preparation for admissions officers, unrealistic text and pictures printed in recruitment pieces, omission of important information for students, and exaggeration of an institution's academic profile and course offerings (Hodum 2007).

2. *Admissions officers should ensure that others who are representing the institution at recruitment events are properly trained and informed with regard to institutional information and ethical behavior.* Frequently, an admissions office calls on alumni, faculty, coaches, and other institutional staff to assist with various events, and these individuals should be informed as to how they should accurately represent the institution and behave in a manner expected by the admissions and recruiting profession. This tenet also came from the *institutional misrepresentation* norm of the NSCARB (Hodum 2007) and stipulates that admissions officers should properly train and inform coaches, alumni, and others who might represent the institution at various recruitment events.

3. *Admissions officers should apply admission requirements in a fair and equitable way, regardless of students' ability to pay.* As institutions struggle to make ends meet, a commitment to helping needy students may erode. A freshman class of students from wealthy homes can seem very promising, but higher education in America has a history of providing access to students from various economic backgrounds. An institution may not have enough funds to help all students; however, admissions officers should apply admission requirements in a way that does not disadvantage needy students solely on their inability to pay. The proscriptive norm of *disregard for the fair treatment of others* gives rise to this tenet, which prohibits discrimination based on students' ability to pay, academic profile, or time of application (Hodum 2007).

4. *Admissions officers should be compensated solely on the basis of salary, without any portion being derived from commissions or bonuses based on numbers of recruited students.* The use of such commissions and bonuses introduced into an officer's compensation suggests to prospective students and their parents that the employee might be looking out for his or her own interests rather than for the interests of the student client. This tenet emanates from the proscriptive norm of *inappropriate compensation.* The specific CARBI behaviors associated with inappropriate compensation include the use of commissions and bonuses paid to admissions officers. (Hodum 2007).

5. *Admissions officers should refrain from paying guidance counselors, coaches, and other like persons for the remuneration of students.* Like the previous tenet, this practice calls into question the commitment of an admissions officer to serve the interests of student clients, and it too stems from the normative pattern of *inappropriate compensation.* The proscriptive behaviors associated with this tenet include the referral payments from admissions officers to others who have influence over prospective students (Hodum 2007).

NEW DIRECTIONS FOR HIGHER EDUCATION • DOI:10.1002/he

6. *Admissions officers should maintain the highest standards of honesty, integrity, and respect for others.* Although this standard is certainly subjective and perhaps ambiguous, it nevertheless is a cornerstone of appropriate ethical behavior. Conduct that causes students, parents, or the general public to question an admissions officer's commitment to this principle will undoubtedly work to undermine the entire profession and erode the trust that is so needed. The proscriptive norm of *dishonest recruitment practices* supplies the foundation for this tenet, and the specific behaviors associated with this norm include an admissions officer shirking responsibility for his or her decisions, as well as an officer taking action that puts colleagues from other institutions at a disadvantage (Hodum 2007).

7. *Admissions officers should maintain strict confidentiality with regard to student information and records.* Although most officers are aware of the requirements set forth in the Family Educational Right to Privacy Act (FERPA), they should go beyond these requirements, as FERPA does not necessarily protect all student data and materials prior to enrollment. Admissions representatives should especially refrain from sharing information with representatives from other institutions. Prospective students certainly have a right to submit this information believing that it will not be shared with other professionals outside the particular institution's admissions office. This tenet is derived from the normative pattern of *breach of confidentiality,* and the behaviors associated with this norm include sharing a student's academic information and offering to trade prospective student lists with admissions representatives from other institutions (Hodum 2007).

8. *Admissions officers should place the interests of students before the interests of their employing institution.* The counseling element of the admissions profession evokes the ideal of service, calling upon admissions officers not to convince a student to choose the officer's employing institution but rather to help them understand themselves and seek the best college fit. The normative pattern of *institutional self-centeredness* provides the basis for this tenet. The behaviors associated with this norm include an officer providing special treatment or opportunities based on nonacademic factors such as family political or financial influence, a student's athletic ability, or a student's ethnicity (Hodum 2007). Although these factors are not necessarily to be disregarded, the idea here is that an officer could focus on how these factors could help his or her employing institution, rather than on the needs of the student client.

9. *Admissions officers should provide full disclosure of admission requirements, deadlines, and costs of attendance.* Officers are not only expected to tell the truth, but to also tell the whole truth. Students deserve to get the full picture of the admission process, timelines, and the expected costs of enrolling at an institution. This tenet emanates from the

normative pattern of *stopping short of full disclosure*. The specific pro-scriptive behaviors aligned with the norm include admissions officers failing to provide enough information to prospective students regarding deadlines, costs, and academic offerings (Hodum 2007).

Higher education commissions and accrediting agencies might certainly want to elaborate on these tenets put forth and develop new ones; however, any additional tenets should continue to meet the three essential characteristics of codes of conduct previously discussed.

Implementing the Code of Conduct

The adoption of a code of conduct by a higher education commission or a regional accrediting body would in and of itself create legitimacy for the code. These governmental bodies and associations are already highly regarded by the higher education community, and they are viewed as holding a certain level of expertise and power. They continually look for ways to develop mechanisms ascertaining the quality assurances at institutions over which they have authority, and the mere development of a code of conduct policy legitimizes the need and action.

One might question, however, the need for a regional accrediting body to adopt such a code of ethics. The mechanisms already in place by these bodies certainly work to ascertain the appropriateness and effectiveness of the various areas within an institution, including the admissions and recruiting offices. The adoption of such a code of ethics would nevertheless augment, not replace, these already-existing evaluation processes. Inclusion of the code in the evaluation of an institution's admission and recruiting policies and practices would work toward providing a clear sense as to why admissions officers should strive for excellence. A code helps keep the focus on student clients, and it provides meaning behind the rules and regulations. Simply put, the code of ethics puts students first.

The following six recommendations for policy and practice could assist higher education commissions and accreditation agencies with the implementation of a code of conduct for admissions and recruiting functions.

1. State higher education commissions and regional accreditation agencies should determine that a developed code of conduct would be required for *all* types of institutions in the state or region—public and private, two-year and four-year, nonprofit and proprietary. Many admissions representatives complain about different rules and different standards held for various types of institutions. One reason that the NACAC and AACRAO codes of conduct have proven less effective at times is because many smaller technical and proprietary schools are not members of these organizations; therefore, any threatened sanctions for violations

of the code are fruitless. Such organizations have the unique opportunity to hold *all* institutions to the same standards, thereby protecting *all* students. The existing NACAC and AACRAO codes of conduct are limited to only those institutions that currently hold membership within these particular associations.

2. State higher education commissions and regional accreditation agencies should establish a mechanism for keeping detailed records regarding reported violations of the code of conduct. Such records should remain confidential to the point allowed by each state's laws and policies. Records should be maintained for at least five years or for at least five years after any sanctions have been met by an institution. The longevity of this information can be critical in identifying repeat offenders, and some states might choose to have no expiration for such information.

3. State higher education commissions and regional accreditation agencies should establish a detailed protocol for investigating allegations of conduct violations. The policies and procedures associated with the investigation process should be clear, concise and thorough, as well as readily available for all to view. This protocol should also be clearly communicated on a regular basis to all institutions under the auspices of the commission and regional accreditation agency.

4. State higher education commissions and regional accreditation agencies should carefully consider and determine the mechanism by which an institution reports a conduct violation. A primary consideration should be whether or not the commission or regional accreditation agency will allow anonymous reporting. The ability to report anonymously might shed more light on problem areas as individuals would be more likely to report infractions knowing they could avoid damaging any professional relationships with other officers or institutions. On the other hand, anonymous reporting might also result in false accusations that could harm the legitimacy of the commission's or regional accreditation agency's entire code of conduct. The commission and accreditation agency should cautiously consider both options and make a decision based on a comprehensive set of factors.

5. State higher education commissions and regional accreditation agencies should determine a specific schedule of sanctions that might result from a variety of conduct infractions. Although this list of sanctions should provide flexibility for the investigating body to make subjective decisions, admissions officers at all institutions should be aware of some specific penalties associated with violating the code of conduct.

6. State higher education commissions and regional accreditation agencies should commit to revisiting the code of conduct on a regular basis, perhaps annually, to make any necessary adjustments. Recruiting techniques, technologies, and strategies are ever changing, and a regular analysis of the code will increase its legitimacy and effectiveness. Admissions professionals should have specific input as to the efficacy of the code and the sanctions associated with its violations.

Conclusion

Many admissions officers across the country might ask why a newly devised code of conduct is necessary. Why are the current codes provided by the National Association of College Admission Counseling and the American Association of Collegiate Registrars and Admission Officers insufficient? Public policy administrators at the various state higher education commissions and accreditation agencies might question the need for their organizations to become involved in the ethics of recruiting and admitting students. These are indeed legitimate questions; however, many admissions officers at a variety of institutions would admit that the recruiting and admission environment has become less fair, honest, and friendly. The codes of conduct provided by NACAC and AACRAO have indeed made a positive impact; however, many complaints revolve around institutions that are not NACAC and AACRAO members and are thus not subject to any sanctions given out by those organizations.

The proliferation of a new code of conduct for recruiting and admissions officers could work to restore trust from students, parents, and the general public. By introducing a code of conduct under the authority of state higher education commissions and accreditation agencies, a broader deployment to all types of institutions will take place, and the problems aligned with limited membership in professional associations will be reduced.

The proposal of a new code of conduct based on normative patterns from empirical research has two main intentions. First, such a code will work toward protecting the student as a client of higher education. With issues such as access, cost, loan repayment, safety, and many others, students and parents certainly need not worry about being taken advantage of by unscrupulous officers who are looking out for their own or their institutions' best interests. Students deserve complete truth, honesty, and fairness from admissions officers. Second, such a code will work toward restoring trust to the profession of admission work. Just as students need not worry about being disadvantaged, admissions officers should be able to carry out their duties while enjoying the confidence of students, parents, and the public.

Many factors, including increased competition, increased greed, and the growth of for-profit education have changed the recruiting and admissions scene in America—many times in a less than positive way. Most officers in the admissions profession work diligently to be respected and trusted. A code of conduct administered through a broad mechanism to cover all types of institutions will grant them the respect and trust they deserve. In addition, adherence to a code of ethics provides freedom and autonomy that these officers desire and need in order to successfully carry out their responsibilities.

NEW DIRECTIONS FOR HIGHER EDUCATION • DOI:10.1002/he

Students deserve to be protected from unethical practices and behaviors. Admissions officers deserve to work in a profession free of suspicion and criticism from the public—a profession honored and respected by others.

References

Barber, B. 1962. *Science and the Social Order*. New York: Collier.

Boyer, E. 1987. *College: The Undergraduate Experience in America*. New York: Harper & Row.

Braxton, J. M. and A. E. Bayer. 1999. *Faculty Misconduct in Collegiate Teaching*. Baltimore: Johns Hopkins University Press.

Braxton, J. M., and A. E. Bayer. 2004. "Toward a Code of Conduct for Undergraduate Teaching." In *Addressing Faculty and Student Classroom Improprieties*, New Directions for Teaching and Learning, no. 99, edited by J. M. Braxton, 47–55. San Francisco: Jossey-Bass.

Carr-Saunders, A. M., and P. A. Wilson. 1933. *The Professions*. Oxford: Clarendon Press.

Gould, A. 2009. "Reauthorizing the Higher Education Act: A Chat with Terry Hartle." *Educause Review,* May–June: 60–61.

Greenwood, E. 1957. "Attributes of a Profession." *Social Work* 2: 44–55.

Grifone-Field, T., M. K. Piersol, and C. Naticchia. 1992. "An Admission Career: How Does It Happen?" *Journal of College Admission*, no. 136: 10–14.

Harries-Jenkins, G. 1970. "Professionals in Organizations." In *Professions and Professionalization*, edited by J. A. Jackson. New York: Cambridge University Press.

Hodum, R. L. 2007. "An Observation of Normative Structure for College Admission and Recruitment Officers." EdD diss., Vanderbilt University.

Hodum, R. L., and G. W. James. 2010. "An Observation of Normative Structure for College Admission and Recruitment Officers." *Journal of Higher Education* 81(3): 317–338.

Johnson, B. 1989. "Student Recruitment: Have We Gone Too Far?" *Journal of College Admissions*, no. 125: 25–28.

Jump, J. W. 1995. "The Ethics of Need-Blind Admission." *Journal of College Admission*, no. 147: 12–15.

McDonough, P., and L. Robertson. 1995. "Reclaiming the Educational Role of Chief Admission Officers." *Journal of College Admission*, no. 147: 22–31.

Millerson, G. 1964. *The Qualifying Associations*. London: Routledge.

Moore, W. E. 1970. *The Professions: Roles and Rules*. New York: Russell Sage Foundation.

ROBERT L. HODUM *is associate vice president for enrollment management and student success at Tennessee Technological University.*

5

Prospective donors and the institutions represented constitute the clients served by college and university fund-raising professionals. This chapter describes nine tenets for a code of conduct for fund-raising professionals that protects the welfare of these clients.

College and University Codes of Conduct for Fund-Raising Professionals

Timothy C. Caboni

Generation of voluntary support for colleges and universities has become an ever more important function that is key to the success of all postsecondary institutions. This is true even for public institutions, which have shifted from primarily focusing on alumni relations activities to executing billion dollar campaigns that equal those conducted by private universities (Kelly 1995). The efforts of community colleges also have begun to include active solicitation of alumni, foundations, and corporations for financial support. At most institutions, the percent of the budget that comes from direct donations is still small but rising, allowing for a few bumps in the economy. For example, in 2008–2009 according to Integrated Postsecondary Education Data System data, gifts accounted for 21 percent of revenues at private, not-for-profit four-year institutions, and almost 4 percent at public four-year institutions. Charitable contributions to colleges and universities in the United States increased 8.2 percent in 2011, reaching $30.30 billion according to results of the annual Voluntary Support of Education survey (Council for Aid to Education 2012).

As development officers generate private support for their institutions, they enjoy great latitude in the approaches they use to solicit individuals for gifts. This professional autonomy is granted to a profession with the expectation that the profession's members will regulate their own behavior and the behavior of their colleagues (Goode 1969).

Goode (1969) suggests that members of a profession must base their individual decisions on what will serve the needs and protect the welfare of their clients. If viewed through this lens, the fund-raising profession has two separate clients for whom it is responsible: the institution and the donor.

NEW DIRECTIONS FOR HIGHER EDUCATION, no. 160, Winter 2012 © Wiley Periodicals, Inc.
Published online in Wiley Online Library (wileyonlinelibrary.com) • DOI:10.1002/he.20035

First, professional fund-raisers are responsible for the welfare of their institutional clients. Development officers are charged with providing necessary capital for the operations of their institutions and for raising money to create endowed funds to provide support for specific projects, programs, scholarships, and professorships in perpetuity (Worth 2002). Along with this responsibility comes the potential for causing great harm to the institution. This harm may be caused in a number of ways, including by entering into agreements that create inappropriate programs for the institution, by poorly representing the university or college to external constituencies, or by misrepresenting what the university or college intends to do with a specific gift.

Second, fund-raisers must protect the individuals who provide funds to their institutions. A development officer could cause harm to institutional supporters in several ways specific to the fund-raising relationship. Two examples include divulging sensitive information about the private financial or personal background of prospects to people outside of the institution or creating planned gifts that are structured in such a way that donors lose access to their accumulated wealth even when those funds are needed (for example, in a health emergency).

Fund-Raising Codes of Conduct

Formal codes of conduct are one way in which a profession helps the behaviors of its members conform to accepted practices (Abbott 1983; Barber 1962; Carr-Saunders and Wilson 1933; Harries-Jenkins 1970). Both of the major professional organizations to which college and university fund-raisers belong, the Council for Advancement and Support of Education (CASE) and the Association of Fundraising Professionals (AFP), have explicitly stated codes of ethics to which their members are expected to conform. Both AFP and CASE also have adopted codes of conduct that apply to their members. CASE adopted the Donor Bill of Rights in 1982. AFP's Code of Ethical Principles was adopted in 1991, and the Principles for Practice were added in 1992. The existence of these codes is an additional marker of professionalism within the field (Braxton and Bayer 1999; Caboni 2010). It should be noted that these are of relatively recent origin compared to the century-old model of modern fund-raising.

However, Kelly (1995) found that less than half (44 percent) of the organizations represented in the National Society of Fundraising Executives (the organization that preceded AFP) had policies regarding the acquisition of gifts and only 50 percent count on professional fund-raisers to abide by a code of professional ethics when receiving gifts or to judge gifts on an individual basis. Lombardo (1991) found that only four of the twelve charitable institutions she studied had formal guidelines to deal with cases of conflict of interest between fund-raisers and donors. In his study of fund-raisers who were members of CASE, Carbone (1989) found that 30 percent of them were unsure if their national organization played a role in setting standards and protecting the right to practice. In addition, he found that "28 percent are unsure if this function is important and 10 percent thought it was unimportant for the organization to do this" (Carbone 1989, 32). In the absence of formal social control mechanisms, fund-raisers must rely upon informal mechanisms to ensure that members of the profession are conforming to what are considered appropriate behaviors. Carlin (1966) and Freidson (1975) found that these informal rules are more important social control mechanisms than formal controls.

Fund-Raising Norms

Norms are one mechanism through which professions self regulate using informal social controls. Norms are shared beliefs about how an individual should act in a particular situation (Merton 1968, 1973). Merton (1957, 1968) suggests that norms function as mechanisms of social control because they consist of prescribed and proscribed patterns of behavior. This concept is derived from Durkheim's (1951) statement that the natural human condition is unregulated passion, whereas conforming requires social regulation. Without a normative structure, individuals in the profession would be free to act as they saw fit, with individuals deciding for themselves what behaviors constituted appropriate and inappropriate behavior. These norms serve as the "collective conscience" of a profession and are another device used by professionals to self-regulate (Braxton and Bayer 1999; Durkheim 1951).

The fund-raising profession possesses a collection of norms that outline for members a set of activities that fund-raisers should avoid during the conduct of their jobs (Caboni 2010). These normative patterns espoused by members of the fund-raising profession establish boundaries that should not be crossed. They were empirically derived through an analysis of survey data collected through the "College Fund Raising Behaviors Inventory," which was administered to professional fund-raisers who were members of CASE (Caboni 2010).

From these analyses, two types of norms emerged: inviolable and admonitory. Norms are considered inviolable when they require the strictest of sanctions when they are violated (Braxton and Bayer 1999). Braxton and Bayer (1999, 44) define norms as admonitory when they "invoke less indignation when violated than inviolable norms."

The fund-raising norms that appear in italics in this paragraph restrict the autonomy development officers have in how they solicit donors (*Unreasonable Enforcement of Pledges* and *Dishonest Solicitation*), how they represent their institutions (*Institutional Disregard*), how they steward university funds (*Exploitation of Institutional Resources* and *Misappropriation of Gifts*), how they persuade prospects to make donations (*Commission-Based Compensation* and *Donor Manipulation*), how they decide for what individuals

NEW DIRECTIONS FOR HIGHER EDUCATION • DOI:10.1002/he

should be solicited (*Institutional Mission Abandonment*), and how they represent themselves professionally (*Exaggeration of Professional Experience*).

Three of these normative patterns emerged as inviolable: *Exploitation of Institutional Resources, Institutional Disregard,* and *Misappropriation of Gifts* (Caboni 2010). The remaining six norms were admonitory in nature: *Commission-Based Compensation, Dishonest Solicitation, Donor Manipulation, Exaggeration of Professional Experience, Institutional Mission Abandonment,* and *Unreasonable Enforcement of Pledges* (Caboni 2010).

Protection of Clients

Goode (1969) suggests that members of a profession must base their individual decisions on what will serve the needs and protect the welfare of their clients. Fund-raising norms protect the interests of both sets of clients for fund-raising professionals. However, the most severe norms protect the fund-raiser's institutional client and the next most serious protect the donor client. The welfare of a fund-raiser's institutional client is protected by all three of the inviolable normative patterns, but donor clients are not protected at all by the inviolable patterns. The admonitory norms are primarily concerned with the welfare of donor clients, with five of the six admonitory norms protecting donors. The only admonitory normative pattern not focused on the welfare of the donor client is institutional mission abandonment, which encompasses the receipt of gifts that the institution does not need or want.

A challenge facing the fund-raising profession is that although the CASE and AFP formal codes of conduct include many of the delineated fund-raising norms, they do not include all of them. The norms that protect the donor are codified in the donor bill of rights adopted by CASE. However, those normative patterns that prohibit transgressions against the fund-raiser's institution are represented in the CASE Statement of Ethics only in generalities. AFP's code of ethical principles is much more thorough in its treatment of inappropriate behaviors. Each of the three inviolable and five of the admonitory norms appear in the code. The admonitory norm against institutional mission abandonment does not appear in any of the discussed codes. This is an example of neglect on the part of the profession to incorporate what are informal norms into the written ethical codes.

Difference Between Junior and Experienced Fund-Raisers

There is a significant difference on several norms between those individuals who have been in the profession for a number of years and those who are new to fund-raising (Caboni 2010). Specifically, those fund-raisers who have been in the profession for no more than three years express significantly less outrage at the violation of the normative array associated with both *Commission-Based Compensation* and *Institutional Mission Abandonment* than those who have been in the profession for fifteen years or more (Caboni 2010). Fund-raisers who have been members of the profession for no more than three years exhibit a lesser degree of disdain for behaviors associated with *Donor Manipulation* than their colleagues who have been in the profession for more than seven years (Caboni 2010).

Institutional Codes of Conduct

Given the gaps in the formal codes adopted by professional fund-raising organizations, higher education institutions might ensure that their development officers understand the boundaries of what comprises appropriate fund-raising behaviors through the creation of institutional codes of conduct. A college code along with an education program intentionally designed to familiarize development staff with its tenets might help prevent the unintentional violation of professional norms. In addition, because the formal codes of conduct used by both CASE and AFP are weighted heavily toward the protection of donor clients, an institutional code could lean toward protection of the organizational client. Also, given the need to socialize new fund-raisers to the profession, and the different levels of disdain espoused on several patterns by those new to the profession as compared to those with more years of experience, those behaviors that should be avoided during the process of cultivating, soliciting, and closing gifts would comprise an important component of an ongoing orientation program. An institutional code also would be a valuable tool to prevent fund-raiser misconduct among all development officers, including those who have been in the profession for a number of years.

Because of this gap in the formal codes, an institution considering the adoption of a local code grounded in the professional norms might include the following prescriptions (the associated proscriptive norm is included along with a description of the norm).

Fund-raisers will at all times be truthful in the solicitation of gifts and transparent with potential donors about how those gifts will be used. Dishonest Solicitation—The normative pattern of *Dishonest Solicitation* proscribes behaviors by fund-raisers that involve untruthfulness while a fund-raiser asks a prospect for a gift.

Fund-raisers will work to have donors fulfill their financial commitments to the institution within the agreed upon span of time and will use good judgment to stop pursuing those commitments when continuing do would damage either the relationship with the donor, or the public perception of the college or university. Unreasonable Enforcement of Pledges—This norm prohibits fund-raisers from taking legal action against a donor or their families in the pursuit of gifts promised to an institution, or from refusing to return a gift made by a donor who is unhappy with how the gift is being used. Although a pledge may be considered a legally binding document, this norm advises fund-raisers and in turn their institutions from pursuing legal action against donors and their families.

Fund-raisers at all times are representatives of the institution for which they work and their actions should reflect positively on the college or university. Institutional Disregard—The normative pattern of *Institutional Disregard* proscribes behaviors by fund-raisers that would damage the reputation of the fund-raiser's employing institution.

Fund-raisers will expend institutional resources in as conservative and frugal a manner as is possible. Exploitation of Institutional Resources—This normative pattern proscribes behaviors by fund-raisers that take advantage of an institution's funds or other things of value that the institution possesses, including offers of admission, for personal gain.

Fund-raisers will ensure that all gifts are used for those purposes the donor originally intended. Misappropriation of Gifts—The inviolable norm regarding *Misappropriation of Gifts* includes transgressions by fund-raisers in which donations are used for purposes that were not intended by the donor. Violation of this normative pattern could cause damage both to the donor client relationship (by misusing the funds given by the individual) and the institutional client (if the donor relationship is compromised because the donation was not used for its intended purpose, the donor might never make another gift to the college).

Fund-raisers will only solicit and cultivate those prospects who have full control of their faculties and are of sound mind. Donor Manipulation—The normative factor dealing with *Donor Manipulation* involves a fund-raiser's handling of delicate relationships with a donor. Individuals who have lost or are losing the capacity to make sound decisions for themselves should not be solicited for gifts. By exploiting these individuals, a fund-raiser is potentially causing harm to the donor client.

Fund-raisers may be compensated with bonuses based upon benchmarks and other goals reached during the course of their work, but may not receive compensation as a percentage of total dollars raised. Commission-Based Compensation—The admonitory norm regarding *Commission-Based Compensation* includes transgressions by fund-raisers in which an individual's salary is paid in part or in full as a percentage of the dollar total raised by that fund-raiser. Violation of this normative pattern is in direct conflict with the code of ethical standards for fund-raisers. The purpose of discouraging these types of compensation packages is to ensure that an individual raising funds for an institution does not take advantage of a donor for financial gain, for example, pushing a donor to make a gift that will do harm to the individual's financial standing because a large gift will result in a large commission.

Fund-raisers will ensure the activities and projects for which they seek funds fit the institution's scope and mission, and will help donors to support those institutional priorities that match their interests. Institutional Mission Abandonment—The behaviors associated with *Institutional Mission*

Abandonment are centered around fund-raisers attracting gifts for things and programs for which the institution has no need. Because fund-raisers are not involved directly in the academic enterprise of the institution, they should not create or change academic programs according to the whim of donors. Doing so infringes upon the institution's autonomy to make programmatic decisions based upon the best interest of enrolled students.

Fund-raisers will describe their background and experience in such a way that those who read the description understand the full extent to which the individual was involved in and responsible for the cultivation, solicitation, and stewardship of any gifts. Exaggeration of Professional Experience—The normative array with respect to *Exaggeration of Professional Experience* centers on fund-raisers who embellish the fund-raising work they have done either at a previous institution or for their current employer.

Conclusion

Socializing new fund-raisers to the profession is key for inculcating norms. Senior fund-raisers, professional organizations, and leaders in the field should consider the benefit of establishing formal mentorships for those individuals who are entering the profession. By developing relationships between beginning fund-raisers and those who have been practicing members of the profession for many years, the profession will increase the chance that those behaviors perceived as inappropriate by those with experience also will be viewed the same way by those who are new. Mentors could be assigned as individuals are hired into an organization. Professional organizations may also engage in this practice.

Given the importance of formal codes of conduct, the ethical code for CASE should have more specific language added to describe fund-raiser responsibility to the institutional client. For example, a proscription might be added that reads, "Even though a donor might want to make a gift for a program with special meaning, if it is not in the best interest of the university to accept that gift, the university should help the donor understand why it might not be helpful to the institution to accept the gift." Another example might include, "Regardless of intent, development officers should avoid any activities that might suggest a gift was made in exchange for something from the university."

The focus of the Donor Bill of Rights is obviously on the welfare of the donor client and specific responsibilities are not delineated for the institutional client. However, it is interesting to note that although an entire document exists outlining the rights of a donor, yet the norms prohibiting behaviors that might cause harm to a donor are almost exclusively in the least severe category. Those norms that proscribe behaviors that place the institution in jeopardy are associated with the most severe sanctions, but the provision of institutional protection in the CASE and AFP codes is scant.

New Directions for Higher Education • DOI:10.1002/he

Finally, as fund-raising continues to grow in its prominence and centrality to higher education, institutions have an important role to play both in safeguarding themselves and helping to move fund-raising toward professionalization. The use of these outlined tenets of a college or university code of conduct would be another step toward that end.

References

Abbott, A. 1983. "Professional Ethics." *American Journal of Sociology* 88(5): 855–885.

Barber, B. 1962. *Science and the Social Order*. New York: Collier.

Braxton, J. M., and A. E. Bayer. 1999. *Faculty Misconduct in Collegiate Teaching*. Baltimore: John Hopkins University Press.

Caboni, T. C. 2010. "The Normative Structure of College and University Fundraising Behaviors." *Journal of Higher Education* 81(3): 339–365.

Carbone, R. F. 1989. *Fundraising as a Profession (Monograph No. 3)*. College Park: University of Maryland, Clearinghouse for Research on Fundraising.

Carlin, J. 1966. *Lawyers' Ethics*. New York: Sage.

Carr-Saunders, A. M., and P. A. Wilson. 1933. *The Professions*. Oxford: Clarendon.

Council for Aid to Education. 2012. *Voluntary Support of Education 2011*. Accessed June 30, 2012. http://vse.cae.org.

Durkheim, E. 1951. *Suicide*. Translated by J. H. Saulding and G. Simpson. New York: Free Press.

Freidson, E. 1975. Doctoring together. A study of professional social control. New York: Elsevier.

Goode, W. J. 1969. "The Theoretical Limits of Professionalization." In *The Semi-Professions and Their Organization*, edited by A. Etzioni. New York: Free Press.

Harries-Jenkins, G. 1970. "Professionals in Organizations." In *Professions and Professionalization*, edited by J. A. Jackson. New York: Cambridge University Press.

Kelly, K. S. 1995. "The Fund-Raising Behavior of U.S. Charitable Organizations." *Journal of Public Relations Research* 7(2): 111–137.

Lombardo, B. J. 1991. "Conflicts of Interest between Nonprofits and Corporate Donors." In *Taking Fund-Raising Seriously: Advancing the Profession and Practice of Raising Money*, edited by D. F. Burlingame and L. J. Hulse. San Francisco: Jossey-Bass.

Merton, R. K. 1957. "Priorities in Scientific Discovery." *American Sociological Review* 2: 635–659.

Merton, R. K. 1968. *Social Theory and Social Structure*. New York: Free Press.

Merton, R. K. 1973. *The Sociology of Science: Theoretical and Empirical Investigations*. Chicago: University of Chicago Press.

Worth, M. J. 2002. *New Strategies for Educational Fundraising*. Phoenix: American Council on Education / Oryx Press.

TIMOTHY C. CABONI is vice chancellor for public affairs at the University of Kansas and holds an appointment as associate professor of educational leadership and policy in the School of Education.

6

This chapter offers a set of six tenets toward a code of conduct to guide the teaching and mentoring of graduate students.

Toward a Code of Conduct for Graduate Education

Eve Proper

Most academic disciplines promulgate codes of ethics that serve as public statements of professional norms of their membership. These codes serve both symbolic and practical purposes, stating to both members and the larger public what a discipline's highest ethics are. Yet these statements vary widely in the range of topics they cover, particularly those that relate to interaction with students, as documented in Braxton, Proper, and Bayer (2011). Many fail to mention students, and those that do focus on the professor as classroom teacher.

This lacuna suggests that working with students is not particularly important to most scholarly society members.[1] It also suggests that dealing with students is limited to traditional coursework, which is only sometimes true for undergraduate faculty and rarely true for graduate faculty (Walker et al. 2008). In advising history professors on how to deal with graduate students, one scholar writes, "Good mentoring involves teaching, advising, criticizing, coaching, cheerleading, challenging, hand-holding, questioning, advocating, nurturing, and, not least, learning and inspiring in both directions" (Cronon 2006, 246). The relationships between faculty and students should be important to any scholarly society whose members are drawn from academia, and the relationship with graduate students ought to be of particular interest. This is not only because the relationship is more intense than at the undergraduate level. Graduate students also learn from their mentors how to be the future of the profession, for good or for ill (Austin 2002; Austin and McDaniels 2006; Braxton, Proper, and Bayer 2011). Scholarly societies have a vested interest in passing on best ethical practices to the next generation of scholars.

This chapter explores what scholarly society codes of ethics could say about the role of graduate faculty. I begin by outlining what we know about norms that pertain to graduate teaching and mentoring and then delineate

NEW DIRECTIONS FOR HIGHER EDUCATION, no. 160, Winter 2012 © Wiley Periodicals, Inc.
Published online in Wiley Online Library (wileyonlinelibrary.com) • DOI:10.1002/he.20036

how these norms could be translated into meaningful, flexible codes of ethics.

What Do Codes of Conduct Say about Faculty–Graduate Student Relations?

In their book, *Professors Behaving Badly*, Braxton, Proper, and Bayer (2011) empirically derived five inviolable and seven admonitory norms for graduate faculty teaching and mentoring. These norms were developed from a survey of faculty in history, biology, chemistry, and psychology on the premise that norms are best recognized when they are violated. The scored items were subjected to factor analysis to create the twelve norms. The authors concluded that graduate faculty do have a shared set of norms for their teaching and mentoring roles, albeit with slight variation by discipline and demographic factors.

The resulting norms were divided into inviolable and admonitory norms based on the strength of disapproval toward violation of them. The inviolable norms, which academics view as warranting severe sanctions, are:

- *Disrespect toward Student Efforts*: This normative pattern proscribes disrespecting the efforts students make in various aspects of their graduate studies. The proscribed behaviors that make up this normative pattern disrespect the efforts of students in the classroom, graded assignments, thesis or dissertation work, and the research apprenticeship.
- *Misappropriation of Student Work*: The failure to give graduate students the credit they deserve for their scholarly efforts typifies this inviolable normative configuration. This particular proscriptive norm demarcates inappropriate behavior of graduate faculty members in their role as "master" in the research apprenticeship for doctoral students.
- *Harassment of Students*: This normative pattern pertains to graduate faculty behaviors that constitute the harassment of students. These proscribed behaviors occur within and outside of the classroom.
- *Whistle-Blowing Suppression*: Whistle-blowing involves the reporting of suspected misconduct by the employer or one of its employees. The inviolable norm of whistle-blowing suppression applies to personally known incidents of scientific misconduct.
- *Directed Research Malfeasance*: This inviolable norm also pertains to incidents of research wrongdoing. In this case, a professor instructs his or her graduate research assistant to engage in wrongdoing.

The admonitory norms, those that academics believe should be avoided but not severely sanctioned, are:

- *Neglectful Teaching*: This array of behaviors refers to behavior that displays a lack of commitment and effort in the role of graduate level of teaching.

NEW DIRECTIONS FOR HIGHER EDUCATION • DOI:10.1002/he

- *Inadequate Advising/Mentoring*: This norm addresses graduate faculty members who counsel or mentor their graduate student advisees in an insufficient manner.
- *Degradation of Faculty Colleagues*: This normative array describes occasions when graduate faculty members disparage their colleagues to other faculty members or to graduate students.
- *Negligent Thesis/Dissertation Advising*: This norm addresses the neglect of faculty responsibilities in supervising the thesis or dissertation work of their graduate students.
- *Insufficient Course Structure*: This normative pattern reminds faculty members to provide sufficient structure to the graduate-level courses they teach.
- *Pedagogical Narrowness*: This normative pattern applies primarily to the content and emphasis of graduate courses. Specifically, this admonitory norm reproves faculty members for choosing a limited pedagogical approach in their graduate courses.
- *Student Assignment Misallocation*: This admonitory norm censures professorial behaviors that put graduate students in awkward positions or misuse their time and efforts.
- *Graduate Program Disregard*: This norm rebukes faculty members who exhibit a lack of concern for the welfare of their graduate program.

Most of these norms are rarely stated explicitly. As part of their research, Braxton, Proper, and Bayer (2011) examined codes of conduct for scholarly societies, both in the four disciplines of the study and in other societies that met Biglan's typology of pure rather than applied (Biglan 1973). They found that "some societies' codes contained no references to students at all" (148), whereas whistle-blowing suppression and directed research malfeasance were rarely addressed even in documents that did touch on students. Most statements regarding students addressed the role of professor as teacher and did not distinguish between graduate and undergraduate students; almost none refer unambiguously to domains more specific to graduate students.

Perhaps this is because the authors of codes of conduct see the codes as opportunities to address the issues particular to that discipline; faculty–student relations are seen as a problem of the professoriate as a whole, not chemists (for example) in particular. Thus, the American Psychological Association's Ethical Principles of Psychologists and Code of Conduct states, "Faculty who are or are likely to be responsible for evaluating students' academic performance do not themselves provide that therapy" (American Psychological Association 2010), a prohibition that would make little sense in most disciplines.

There were exceptions. For example, the American Historical Association's code of ethics states, "teachers of graduate seminars are critical in shaping a young historian's perception of the ethics of scholarship. It is therefore incumbent on graduate teachers to seek opportunities for making the seminar also a workshop in scholarly integrity" (American Historical Association 2011).

Notably—although this was outside the scope of our project—codes of conduct had little to say about service or administrative duties. The admonitory norm of *Graduate Program Disregard* could best be described as falling into this area. This neglect of administrative duties in general could be a lifetime of research in and of itself, but for the present it is sufficient to note that all faculty have administrative duties, no matter whether they are involved primarily in graduate or undergraduate teaching, and the invisibility of this is both interesting and complex.

Why Should Codes of Conduct Address the Relations of Graduate Faculty and Students?

Why is it problematic that codes of ethics fail to address faculty interactions with graduate students? First, there is evidence that improprieties occur. Stories in the *Chronicle of Higher Education, Inside Higher Ed*, and even the general press report cases of students pressured to suppress whistle-blowing, student plagiarism aided by faculty, and sexual harassment of students. The academic press and blogosphere contain firsthand accounts of indifferent and neglectful faculty members and stories of misappropriated work. Few of these cases are reported or handled in a formal way, making it difficult to document the extent of these behaviors, but anecdotal evidence suggests that they occur.

Second, codes are a key place to strengthen academic norms. Many of them are explicitly used as signals rather than enforceable rules, as, for example, the American Historical Society's decision to stop adjudicating cases of plagiarism (Bartlett 2003). As highly symbolic documents, codes of ethics exist first and foremost as statements of professional norms, and it is only appropriate that they document the full extent of professional activity. In particular, codes provide a platform for graduate students to learn about their disciplines' norms. This is beneficial both for socializing them as future members of the professoriate and for informing them of their rights as students.

Third, discipline-specific codes are the appropriate place to address issues that vary in salience by discipline. Academics have long recognized that there are differences between academic disciplines, many of which are the result of research methods (Braxton and Hargens 1996). Although the norms applied across all four disciplines studied, Braxton, Proper, and Bayer's (2011) study found differences in their strength. This is not to suggest that similar attention to graduate faculty ethics would be inappropriate in other places, such as institutional codes of conduct. Nevertheless, especially for "cosmopolitan" faculty, disciplinary societies often provide a primary point of identification. Cosmopolitan faculty are those who identify primarily with their discipline, which has a national or international scope, rather than with their particular campus (Gouldner 1957).

What Would a Code of Conduct for Faculty–Graduate Student Relations Address?

Inasmuch as codes of conduct address either the undergraduate or the unspecified "student," most extant references are appropriate to dealings with graduate students. They tend to address the following (Braxton, Proper, and Bayer 2011):

- General "respect"
- Sexual harassment and relationships
- Classroom behaviors

The norms governing these areas, at least insofar as they are loosely formulated in codes of conduct, do not vary significantly between undergraduates and graduate students. What these codes fail to address is that the faculty–student relationship extends far beyond the classroom and beyond a faculty members role in advising and sponsoring student clubs and organizations, which faculty often do for undergraduates. The faculty–graduate student relationship also includes the roles of supervisor, mentor, and dissertation or thesis supervisor.

It is possible for all of these roles to occur at the undergraduate level, but those cases are less common, less intense, and less critical for future career success.

The Graduate Faculty Member as Teacher

To the extent that codes of conduct address faculty roles, they focus on the faculty member as teacher. For faculty who do not teach graduate students, this comprises the bulk of their workload. Even for graduate faculty, this is not a negligible role, either in terms of time or importance. Unsurprisingly, two of the inviolable norms for graduate education fall into this area: *Disrespect toward Student Efforts* and *Misappropriation of Student Work*. Several of the admonitory norms address this area as well: *Neglectful Teaching, Insufficient Course Structure,* (most of) *Pedagogical Narrowness,* and *Student Assignment Misallocation*.

The Graduate Faculty Member as Supervisor

Full-time graduate students often work for faculty members as either teaching assistants or research assistants. In 2009, 61.6 percent of male and 57.2 percent of female doctoral recipients had earned funds from teaching assistantships, and 63.9 percent of male and 53.8 percent of female recipients had earned funds from research assistantships, according to the National

Science Foundation's (2009) Survey of Earned Doctorates. Assisting with teaching is a role unique to graduate students and, as such, is nearly absent in all codes of conduct. Supervision of research assistants, however, is different only in degree from research supervision of permanent employees, which is particularly common in the sciences. Many—but not all—of the behaviors included in *Misappropriation of Student Work* are related to research supervision. (Exceptions include routinely borrowing money from graduate student advisees and accepting costly gifts from graduate students.) All of the behaviors in *Whistle-blowing Suppression* and *Directed Research Malfeasance* belong here, as do some aspects of the admonitory norm of *Student Assignment Misallocation*.

The Graduate Faculty Member as Mentor

Although the term "advisor" is typically used, this may conjure up someone whose primary role is to aid a student in choosing courses along with providing occasional career advice. In reality, the advisor–graduate student relationship is much richer than this, as suggested by Cronon (2006). The faculty member has a role in socializing the student not only to the institution but also to the discipline and the larger world of academia (Austin and McDaniels 2006; Golde 2006) and, in the case of some international students, to life in the United States. They truly serve as mentors, guiding students on everything from what kind of experience will best position the student in the academic job market to what is appropriate attire at a professional conference. Winston and Polkosnik (1984) call this role "occupational socializer."

The mentoring role is made more complex by the fact that, as Bucher and Stelling (1977) have shown in medical education, students have multiple mentors. It is rare for a student to find one faculty member who has similar research and methodological interests, has recently been on the job market, and is able to address issues that arise related to race, gender, or nationality. Rockquemore (2011) addresses the issue of faculty needing multiple mentors, but the issue is equally salient for graduate students.

Many of the behaviors described by the admonitory norm of *Inadequate Advising/Mentoring* belong here. Many of the varied behaviors described by *Degradation of Faculty Colleagues* could find a home here as well.

The Graduate Faculty Member as Thesis Supervisor

Faculty members supervise student theses, a role that differs significantly from ordinary classroom teaching or even overseeing independent study. Faculty members are notoriously variable in their fulfillment of that role, even within the same department and institution. As Fox (2000, 57) has pointed out, even individual "departments leave untouched the core of graduate education: the advisor-advisee relationship" and rarely regulate the relationship between advisor and advisee. Common areas of disagreement revolve around when the proposal defense should occur and how often or how fast feedback is provided.

There are unavoidable academic disciplinary differences that place some parameters on the unearthing of best practices. Students who work in laboratories as part of large teams will have fundamentally different experiences than students in the humanities who typically conduct solitary research. Thus, we would expect disciplinary codes of conduct to reflect the nature of research in their respective disciplines.

The norm of *Negligent Thesis/Dissertation Advising* clearly fits here. Some of the behaviors described by the admonitory norms of *Inadequate Advising/Mentoring* and *Student Assignment Misallocation* also belong here.

What Would a Code of Conduct for Graduate Faculty Look Like?

A code of conduct for faculty, whether part of a general code or a specific document, could be organized in several ways. One option would be to address each of the norms established by Braxton et al. (2011). Although I certainly would not discourage such use of this work, what is more important is that the breadth of faculty's work with graduate students be acknowledged. A simpler model would be for codes of conduct to discuss the varying roles of faculty in the relevant discipline—teacher, mentor, supervisor, thesis chair, *and* researcher, not to mention service provider. Although not all members of any scholarly society take on all of these roles, the alternative—to ignore all of these except researcher and perhaps teacher, as most of them do now—is a greater disservice to an organization's membership. Nevertheless, there are some pitfalls to watch out for:

- *Narrowness versus generality.* If some codes of conduct tend to be too general, it is also possible to swing the pendulum too far in the opposite direction. For example, codes of conduct mandating that finished syllabi be ready on the first day of class leave no room for faculty to engage their students in cocreating a course syllabus as a thoughtful, planned in-course activity with a pedagogical purpose. Moreover, overly long ethical codes are unlikely to be read and may feel like legalistic traps. There will always be a tension between too much and not enough specificity.
- *"But do we need to say it?"* One might argue that the inclusion of specific behaviors implies others that are not directly mentioned. For example, if a code addresses the importance of presenting data accurately and honestly, is it necessary to state that one should not tell others to falsify data? There is some merit to this argument, and a code that ended every sentence with, "and don't tell others to do it, either," would make for tedious reading. Nevertheless, this can be approached more obliquely, as in the newest version of the American Educational Research Association

(AERA) Code of Ethics: "Education researchers provide proper training and supervision to their students, and take reasonable steps to see that such persons perform services responsibly, competently, and ethically" (155). Particularly when coupled with an acknowledgement of the dependency and vulnerability of the master-apprentice relationship, this type of language provides an efficient means of covering much territory.

- *Repetition:* Some faculty responsibilities toward graduate students are similar if not identical to their responsibilities toward undergraduates. Therefore, not all need to be addressed to graduate faculty explicitly. For example, a code could address faculty relations with students in general, and then address particular issues with graduate and undergraduate populations separately. Although norms are different for undergraduates and graduates (not to mention professional degrees, which we have not addressed), strong commonalities exist and it may be appropriate to address faculty relations with "students." For example, a code could simply prohibit sexual or romantic relationships between faculty and *all* students, or mandate the use of syllabi. Nearly all the behaviors under *Disrespect toward Student Efforts,* for example, are classroom related and could be discussed without respect to student level. The norm of *Harassment of Students* includes behavior both in and out of the classroom, but again could be addressed in a level-neutral way.

With these caveats in mind, what follows is a model for a code of conduct for graduate faculty. It addresses each of the four roles—teacher, supervisor, mentor, and thesis supervisor—as well as university service related to students and general responsibilities that inhere across roles.

A Sample Scholarly Society Code for Graduate Faculty

1. A faculty member respects students as individuals, while recognizing that the faculty–student relationship inherently gives more power to the faculty member. A faculty member does not take advantage of a student's subordinate status by a) engaging in sexual relationships with him or her, b) presenting a student's work as the faculty member's own, or c) requesting personal favors. A faculty member safeguards the interests of current and future students by a) not admitting inadequately prepared students to the graduate degree program, and by b) not requiring current students to take on responsibilities beyond their capabilities.

2. A faculty member takes his or her instructional responsibilities seriously and treats students with respect and without favoritism. A faculty member a) designs courses in a thoughtful way and explains the course structure to students, b) respects and rewards student thought and expression, c) accurately assesses student learning in a timely and objective manner, d) respects student time and attention, and

e) accurately presents the breadth and depth of the subject regardless of his or her specialty or beliefs.

3. A faculty member is a responsible supervisor to all employees and recognizes that some employees, such as graduate students, are particularly dependent. A faculty member a) holds students responsible for their work while recognizing that they are apprentices rather than experts, b) demonstrates and expects the highest safety and ethical standards, and c) encourages student employees to report research misconduct.

4. A faculty member is a responsible mentor to his or her students and recognizes that mentoring is an activity that requires the cooperation of multiple faculty members. A faculty member a) endeavors to understand and accurately impart program requirements; b) holds all students to program standards; c) encourages students to learn from other faculty members when appropriate; d) provides professional development, including introductions, letters of recommendation, and career advice; e) does not take on more advisees than he or she has time to advise well; and f) adapts tasks to student experience and learning.

5. A faculty member devotes time and attention to student theses, particularly those for which he or she serves as chair. A faculty member a) encourages students to complete the thesis and graduate in a timely manner; b) encourages students to work independently in regard to methods, research questions, and subsequent publications; c) provides substantive and timely advice and feedback; and d) prepares students for successful defense of their work.

6. A faculty member devotes time and energy to service to the institution and the discipline. With regard to students, this includes participating in decisions on a) the admissions process and requirements, and b) program content and structure.

Note that this code is not specific about some of these provisions. Is "timely advice and feedback" on a thesis given within one week, four weeks, or two months of receiving a draft? Possibly, a code could be so specific. However, such agreement could be reached only after long dialog within a discipline. I suggest this model with the expectation that it would be modified to meet the needs of particular disciplines, such as the role of therapy in psychology, the intensive one-on-one work in music, and the large team research model in some of the hard sciences. Individual disciplines would benefit from surveying their members to find out more about their normative orientation.

Conclusion

Developing codes of conduct for faculty graduate student interactions would, in the long run, improve the mentee experience of all graduate students, as well as help faculty members who are anxious to understand their role. In the short term, disciples would benefit from frank and open dialog about what the standards should be. At a time when the professoriate is undergoing structural changes and there is widespread discussion about the graduate school experience, this is a worthwhile conversation to begin.

Note

1. It is true that some organizations may have a high percentage of members who are not professors, particularly in the sciences.

References

American Historical Association. 2011. "Statement on Standards of Professional Conduct." Accessed April 15, 2012. http://www.historians.org/pubs/Free/Professional Standards.cfm.

American Psychological Association. 2010. "Ethical Principles of Psychologists and Code of Conduct." Accessed April 15, 2012. http://www.apa.org/ethics/code/index .aspx.

Austin, A. E. 2002. "Preparing the Next Generation of Faculty: Graduate School as Socialization to the Academic Career." *Journal of Higher Education* 73(1): 94–122.

Austin, A. E., and M. McDaniels. 2006. "Preparing the Professoriate of the Future: Graduate Student Socialization for Faculty Roles." In *Higher Education: Handbook of Theory and Research*, Vol. 21, edited by J. C. Smart. New York: Springer.

Bartlett, T. 2003. "Historical Association Will No Longer Investigate Allegations of Wrongdoing." *Chronicle of Higher Education*, May 23: A12.

Biglan, A. 1973. "The Characteristics of Subject Matter in Different Academic Areas." *Journal of Applied Psychology* 57: 195–203.

Braxton, J. M., and L. Hargens. 1996. "Variation among Academic Disciplines: Analytical Frameworks and Research." In *Higher Education: Handbook of Theory and Research*, Vol. 11, edited by J. C. Smart. New York: Agathon Press.

Braxton, J. M., E. Proper, and A. E. Bayer. 2011. *Professors Behaving Badly: Faculty Misconduct in Graduate Education*. Baltimore: Johns Hopkins University Press.

Bucher, R., and J. G. Stelling. 1977. *Becoming Professional*. Vol. 46. Beverly Hills: Sage Publications.

Cronon, W. 2006. "Getting Ready to Do History." In *Envisioning the Future of Doctoral Education: Preparing Stewards of the Discipline: Carnegie Essays on the Doctorate*, edited by C. M. Golde, G. E. Walker, and Associates. San Francisco: Jossey-Bass.

Fox, M. 2000. "Organizational Environments and Doctoral Degrees Awarded to Women in Science and Engineering Departments." *Women's Studies Quarterly* 28(1): 47–61.

Golde, C. M. 2006. "Preparing Stewards of the Discipline." In *Envisioning the Future of Doctoral Education: Preparing Stewards of the Discipline: Carnegie Essays on the Doctorate*, edited by C. M. Golde, G. E. Walker, and Associates. San Francisco: Jossey-Bass.

Gouldner, A. W. 1957. "Cosmopolitans and Locals: Toward an Analysis of Latent Social Roles." *Administrative Science Quarterly* 2(3): 281–306.

National Science Foundation. 2009. *2009 Survey of Earned Doctorates*. Accessed July 19, 2011. http://www.nsf.gov/statistics/nsf11306/.

Rockquemore, K. A. 2011. "Don't Talk about Mentoring." *Inside Higher Ed.* Accessed August 28, 2012. http://www.insidehighered.com/advice/mentoring/debut_of_new_column_on_mentoring_in_higher_education_careers.

Walker, G. E., C. M. Golde, L. Jones, A. C. Bueschel, and P. Hutchings. 2008. *Formation of Scholars: Rethinking Doctoral Education for the Twenty-First Century*. San Francisco: Jossey-Bass.

Winston, R. B., Jr., and M. B. Polkosnik. 1984. "Advising Graduate and Professional School Students." In *Developmental Academic Advising: Addressing Students' Educational, Career, and Personal Needs*, edited by R. B. Winston, T. K. Miller, S. C. Ender, T. J. Grites, and Associates. San Francisco: Jossey-Bass.

Eve Proper is an assistant professor of management at LIM College. She earned a PhD in higher education leadership and policy at Vanderbilt University.

7

This chapter reports the findings of a study conducted to determine the existence of codes of conduct for undergraduate college teaching in public and private colleges and universities that espouse a teaching-oriented mission.

The Existence of Codes of Conduct for Undergraduate Teaching in Teaching-Oriented Four-Year Colleges and Universities

Dawn Lyken-Segosebe, Yunkyung Min, John M. Braxton

Four-year colleges and universities that espouse teaching as their primary mission bear a responsibility to safeguard the welfare of their students as clients of teaching. This responsibility takes the form of a moral imperative.

Faculty members hold considerable autonomy in the professional choices they make in their teaching (Braxton and Bayer 1999). As a consequence, institutionally based codes of conduct are needed to provide guidelines for those choices. Such professional choices include course planning and course design, communication with a class, grading criteria for examinations and other assignments, and in-class relationships with students (Braxton and Bayer 1999, 2004). For example, choices in course design and planning, such as not preparing a course syllabus or changing the meeting time of the class without consulting students, can result in students getting behind in their readings and course assignments. Treating students with disrespect and in a condescending manner is an aspect of communication with a class that can harm student learning. The awarding of grades based on criteria other than merit can harm the future academic performance and careers of students. Without guidelines that safeguard student welfare in the classroom, faculty members may make unconstrained and idiosyncratic choices in their teaching performance that may have a negative impact on students as clients (Braxton and Bayer 1999).

A key question emerges: As a way to safeguard student welfare in the classroom, do teaching-oriented four-year colleges and universities

NEW DIRECTIONS FOR HIGHER EDUCATION, no. 160, Winter 2012 © Wiley Periodicals, Inc.
Published online in Wiley Online Library (wileyonlinelibrary.com) • DOI:10.1002/he.20037

promulgate codes of conduct for undergraduate teaching? This chapter addresses this question by reviewing results of a research study to determine the existence and public dissemination of such codes of conduct.

Conceptual Framework

Four-year teaching-oriented colleges and universities constitute an organizational field within the system of colleges and universities in the United States. This particular organizational field includes those colleges and universities classified as "Baccalaureate Colleges" in the Carnegie Classification of Institutions (Carnegie Foundation 2010). Within each organizational field an institutional environment exists that consists of norms and values influencing the behavior of organizations within that particular organizational field. Stakeholders' perceptions of specific organizations as trustworthy and legitimate result from the organizations' adherence to the norms and values of their institutional environments (Zucker 1987).

Adherence to the norms and values of an institutional environment occurs because of isomorphism among those teaching colleges and universities that comprise the Baccalaureate Colleges category of the Carnegie Classification of Institutions (2010). Isomorphism pertains to the similarity in values and norms espoused by the specific organizations within an institutional environment of an organizational field (DiMaggio and Powell 1983). Mimetic Isomorphism and Normative Isomorphism constitute types of isomorphism relevant in the case of teaching-oriented colleges and universities.

Mimetic Isomorphism refers to the intentional imitation or copying of other organizations in order to shape perceptions of trustworthiness and legitimacy among organizational stakeholders (DiMaggio and Powell 1983). Relevant stakeholders for teaching-oriented colleges and universities include the prospective students and their parents, enrolled students and their parents, members of the institution's board of trustees, and the administration, faculty, staff, and alumni.

Normative Isomorphism pertains to the process by which organizations gradually acquire the norms and values operative in other organizations within their particular institutional environment. This form of isomorphism takes place through the hiring of administrators, faculty, and staff from other teaching-oriented colleges and universities. Normative isomorphism may also occur through institutional participation in various associations of teaching-oriented colleges and universities (DiMaggio and Powell 1983).

These formulations suggest two possibilities regarding the existence of codes of conduct for undergraduate teaching at four-year teaching-oriented colleges and universities: Their existence is either rare or prevalent within this organizational field. Either mimetic or normative isomorphism can result in either state of the existence of codes of conduct for undergraduate college teaching. To elaborate, if few institutions promulgate such codes, then most other teaching-oriented colleges and universities will not promulgate such codes. Either mimetic or normative isomorphism will result in the rarity of such codes. If many teaching-oriented colleges publicly declare codes of conduct, then many other teaching-oriented colleges and universities will also do so. Either mimetic or normative isomorphism will result in the prevalence of such codes. The methodologies employed in a given study will determine which form of isomorphism—mimetic or normative—appears to exert an influence. However, the methodology we used in this study does not permit us to make such a determination.

Methodology

Braxton and Bayer (2004) proposed a formal code of conduct for undergraduate college teaching that colleges and universities could implement to deter the practice of improprieties by faculty members. The code of conduct comprises ten tenets that reflect a set of norms safeguarding the welfare of students by proscribing inappropriate faculty behavior related to undergraduate teaching. Braxton and Bayer (1999) empirically derived these norms from the perceptions of faculty members at a full spectrum of colleges and universities (research universities, comprehensive colleges and universities, liberal arts colleges, and two-year colleges). The ten tenets are listed in Table 7.1 with examples of evidence of their existence and the proscriptive norms to which each tenet is related.

To assess whether teaching-oriented four-year colleges and universities promulgate codes of conduct for undergraduate teaching, we undertook a content analysis of the websites of Baccalaureate Colleges offering arts and sciences programs. We sought evidence for each of the ten tenets of the code of conduct proposed by Braxton and Bayer (2004).

Sample and Data Collection. The 287 institutions designated as Baccalaureate Colleges offering arts and sciences programs within the Carnegie Foundation (2010) Basic Classification served as the population of inference. One hundred institutions were randomly selected from this group of baccalaureate colleges: 38 public institutions and 62 private not-for-profit institutions. The websites of each of the 100 institutions were searched using the key words "faculty handbook," "faculty guide," "employee guide," and "code of conduct."

We delineated an additional tenet during the research process. Frequent referencing in institutional policy documents suggested that the tenet *Harassment* was indicated for a code of conduct for undergraduate college teaching. Its meaning is adopted from Colgate University's Harassment Policy which defines *Harassment* in terms of "oral, written, graphic, or physical conduct that is sufficiently severe, persistent, or pervasive so as to interfere with or limit the ability of an individual to participate in or benefit from programs or activities" (Colgate University Faculty Handbook 2012, 49). This eleventh tenet is related to the proscriptive norm of moral turpitude.

Table 7.1 Tenets Required of an Undergraduate College Code of Conduct

#	Tenet	Evidence	Corresponding Proscriptive Faculty Norm
1.	Undergraduate courses should be carefully planned.	Textbooks and course materials ordered in time Adequate course outline and syllabus prepared Dates for assignments and exams	Inattentive planning Insufficient syllabus
2.	Important course details should be conveyed to enrolled students.	Office hours Class attendance policy Changes in class time or location Reading assignments Opportunities for extra credit Grading criteria for essays on exams or papers Policy on missed or makeup exam	Uncommunicated course details Inadequate communication
3.	New and revised lectures and course readings should reflect advancements of knowledge in a field.	Keep up to date with advancement of knowledge in their academic discipline	Inadequate course design
4.	Grading of examinations and assignments should be based on merit and not on the characteristics of students.	Grades not affected by personal friendships No preferential treatment for late work, incompletes, and opportunities for extra-credit work	Particularistic grading
5.	Various perspectives on course topics should be presented, examinations should cover the breadth of the course, and scholars' or students' perspectives at variance with the instructor's point of view should be acknowledged.	Various perspectives presented Student perspective at variance with instructor's point of view acknowledged Exams cover breadth of course	Authoritarian classroom Instructional narrowness

6.	Students should be treated with respect as individuals.	Students not treated condescendingly or in a demeaning way; needs and sensitivities of students respected	Condescending negativism Personal disregard
		Classes not routinely dismissed early Instructors not routinely late for class meetings Patience with slow learners	Inconvenience avoidance
7.	Faculty members must respect the confidentiality of their relation-ships with students and the students' academic achievements.	Respect confidentiality of relationship Respect confidentiality of students' academic accomplishments	
8.	Faculty members must make themselves available to their students by maintaining office hours.	Maintain office hours Be prepared for student advising Be prepared to identify special services to deal with student problems outside faculty expertise	Advisement negligence
9.	Faculty members must not have sexual relationships with students enrolled in their classes.	No sexual relationships with enrolled students Refrain from making sexual comments to students	Moral turpitude
10.	Faculty members must not come to class intoxicated from alcohol or drugs.	No use of alcohol or drug on campus	Moral turpitude

Note: This table is constructed from Braxton and Bayer (2004), 49–51.

Findings

There were 100 liberal arts colleges and universities in our sample—38 public and 62 private institutions. We found references to the defined tenets in 78 institutions—33 public institutions (86.8 percent) and 45 private institutions (72.6 percent). The percentages displayed in Tables 7.2, 7.3, and 7.4 are based on those institutions that had at least one tenet rather than on the total number of institutions in the sample.

The content analysis of institutional websites reveals that the most prevalent tenets concern moral turpitude: *Faculty members must not have sexual relationships with students enrolled in their classes* (tenet 9) and *Faculty members must not come to class intoxicated from alcohol or drugs* (tenet 10). The faculty handbooks in 61 percent of private and 84 percent of public colleges stipulate that faculty members not engage in sexual relationships with enrolled students whereas 48 percent of private colleges and 76 percent of public liberal arts colleges state that faculty members must not come to class intoxicated from alcohol or drugs.

Other prevalent tenets are *Faculty members must respect the confidentiality of their relationships with students and the students' academic achievements* (tenet 7) and *Faculty members must make themselves available to their students by maintaining office hours* (tenet 8). Thus, faculty members in 40 percent of private colleges and 71 percent of public colleges are requested to refrain from engaging in the proscriptive norm of inconvenience avoidance whereas 44 percent of private colleges and 68 percent of public colleges state that faculty must not practice advisement negligence.

The tenets receiving the least coverage on institutional websites are *New and revised lectures and course readings should reflect advancements of knowledge in a field* (tenet 3) and *Grading of examinations and assignments should be based on merit and not on the characteristics of students* (tenet 4). We found reference to tenet 3 regarding the necessity for adequate course design in only 16 percent of private institutions and 42 percent of public institutions. Merit-based grading is the second least common tenet because 21 percent of private institutions and 45 percent of public institutions refer to tenet 4. Tenet 11, *Harassment*, is mentioned on the websites of half of the colleges in our sample.

Although most of these institutions promulgate at least six tenets, we find greater evidence of tenets on the websites of public than private liberal arts colleges and universities. Tables 7.2 and 7.3 indicate the prevalence of tenets by type of institution.

We also conducted *t*-tests between public and private institutions on each of the eleven tenets as the percentage distributions exhibited in Table 7.3 may be due to chance. We observe from Table 7.4 that the percentage differences between public and private teaching-oriented colleges and universities are due to chance for tenets 5, 6, and 11. In contrast, we note that the percentage differences between private and public institutions are

Table 7.2 Prevalence of Tenets by Institutional Type and Number of Tenets

Number of Tenets	Private Institutions (%)	Public Institutions (%)
1	13	0
2–5	33	18
6–10	47	72
11	7	9

Table 7.3 Percentages of Institutions with Each of Eleven Tenets of the Undergraduate College Code of Conduct

Tenet	Private Institutions (%)	Public Institutions (%)	Total (%)
1. Attentive planning	29	74	46
2. Course details should be conveyed	24	68	41
3. Adequate course design	16	42	26
4. Merit-based grading	21	45	30
5. Various perspectives presented	30	42	35
6. Students should be treated with respect as individuals	34	47	39
7. Respect confidentiality of relationship	40	71	52
8. Maintain office hours	44	68	53
9. No sexual relationships	61	84	70
10. No use of alcohol or drugs	48	76	59
11. No harassment	52	50	51

statistically significant at the .05 level for eight of the eleven tenets (1, 2, 3, 4, 7, 8, 9, and 10). Put differently, we find that public four-year teaching-oriented colleges and universities tend to promulgate these eight tenets to a greater extent than do private four-year teaching-oriented colleges and universities.

Limitations

Three limitations temper our conclusions and recommendations for institutional action and future research. The first limitation pertains to the breadth of information an institution may provide on its website. An institution may have policies related to the eleven tenets, but may provide only some (or none) of these policies on its website. It is also possible that policies related to faculty conduct are accessible only to the institution's faculty and staff members.

A second limitation derives from the key words used in the search process. These key words may not match the terminology used by

New Directions for Higher Education • DOI:10.1002/he

Table 7.4 Results of *t*-Test for Each of Eleven Tenets by Institution Type

Tenet	Type of Institution	Obs	Mean	Std. Err.	Std. Dev.	t-test
1. Attentive planning	Private	62	.290	.058	.458	−4.781***
	Public	38	.736	.072	.446	
2. Course details should be conveyed	Private	62	.242	.055	.432	−4.802***
	Public	38	.684	.076	.471	
3. Adequate course design	Private	62	.161	.047	.371	−2.971**
	Public	38	.421	.081	.500	
4. Merit-based grading	Private	62	.210	.052	.410	−2.575*
	Public	38	.447	.082	.504	
5. Various perspective presented	Private	62	.306	.059	.465	−1.162
	Public	38	.421	.081	.500	
6. Respect for students	Private	62	.339	.061	.477	−1.342
	Public	38	.474	.082	.506	
7. Respect confidentiality of relationship	Private	62	.403	.063	.495	−3.097**
	Public	38	.711	.075	.460	
8. Maintain office hours	Private	62	.435	.063	.500	−2.468*
	Public	38	.684	.076	.471	
9. No sexual relationships	Private	62	.613	.062	.491	−2.477*
	Public	38	.842	.060	.370	
10. No use of alcohol or drugs	Private	62	.484	.064	.504	− 2.839**
	Public	38	.763	.070	.431	
11. No harassment	Private	62	.516	.064	.504	0.155
	Public	38	.500	.082	.507	

*p < 0.05, **p < 0.01, ***p < 0.001

institutions on their websites. Stronger inferences about the tendency of four-year colleges and universities to promulgate codes of conduct for undergraduate teaching may require e-mail or telephonic confirmation from institutional administration.

Our inability to determine whether our findings resulted from mimetic or normative isomorphism constitutes a third limitation of this study. Our methodology of using the websites of each of the 100 institutions selected prevented us from measuring the apparent influence of these two forms of isomorphism.

Conclusions

We conclude that isomorphic pressures within the organizational field, four-year teaching-oriented colleges and universities, result in the tendency of the majority of the institutions in this field to copy—intentionally or unintentionally—their institutional counterparts in this organizational field by publicly posting on their websites codes of conduct for undergraduate teaching. This conclusion stems from our finding that faculty handbooks and other relevant documents in the vast majority of four-year private and public institutions refer to at least one tenet with the preponderance of institutions referencing six to ten tenets.

We also conclude that the organizational field of teaching-oriented colleges and universities is segmented by institutional control. Put differently, isomorphic pressures for institutionally promulgated undergraduate teaching codes of conduct appear stronger in public teaching-oriented four-year institutions than in private four-year institutions espousing a teaching mission. Our finding that public four-year teaching-oriented institutions tend to designate eight of the eleven tenets to a greater degree than their privately controlled counterparts supports this conclusion.

Recommendations for Institutional Action and Future Research

Faculty violations of the tenets of institutional codes of conduct constitute teaching misconduct (Braxton and Bayer 2004). Because these tenets safeguard the welfare of students as clients of undergraduate college teaching, teaching misconduct requires social control (Braxton and Bayer 2004; Braxton, Bayer, and Noseworthy 2004). Social control entails the mechanisms of deterrence, detection, and sanctioning (Zuckerman 1988). Without codes of conduct, the deterrence, detection, and sanctioning of teaching improprieties is problematic. As a consequence, we recommend that those public and private teaching-oriented colleges and universities that currently do not promulgate any of the eleven tenets identified in this study develop codes of conduct for undergraduate college teaching. The isomorphic pressures of their organizational field strongly suggest the need for the development of such codes. We likewise recommend that colleges and universities in other organizational fields defined by institutional mission develop codes of conduct for undergraduate college teaching.

To such individual colleges and universities we offer two additional recommendations that echo those advanced by Braxton and Bayer (2004) regarding their proposed code of conduct for undergraduate teaching. These recommendations are as follows:

1. Institutions should maintain official records of reported violations of the tenets of their codes of conduct for undergraduate college teaching. In addition to offering this recommendation, Braxton and Bayer (2004) also suggested that such official records also contain such information as whether an investigation of the reported incident took place and the outcome of this investigation.
2. Institutions should create teaching integrity committees. According to Braxton and Bayer (2004), teaching integrity committees should consider reported incidents of violations of the tenets of institutional codes of conduct for undergraduate college teaching. We concur with their suggestion that such committees should develop methods for undergraduate students to report such incidents with ease. We also concur with their strong assertion that the procedures used by such a committee in conducting its investigation should protect both the accused faculty member and the individual making the allegation.

In addition to these recommendations for institutional policy, we also recommend four areas for future research on institutional codes of undergraduate college teaching. These four recommendations are as follows:

1. The current study was unable to ascertain whether mimetic or normative isomorphism exerted an influence in producing the findings of this study. Future research should be conducted to determine which form of isomorphism tends to prevail within the organizational field of teaching-oriented colleges and universities.
2. The current study should be replicated in other organizational fields defined by particular types of colleges and universities. The organizational fields of two-year community colleges and research-oriented universities present settings for such research. These two organizational fields represent extremes in terms of organizational missions. Such research should make distinctions between public and private institutions in these organizational fields.
3. We also recommend that such studies address such questions as: Are teaching integrity committees in existence? Are allegations of teaching misconduct handled by other institutional committees? Are the possible sanctions for teaching misconduct that a teaching integrity committee may recommend publicly delineated in institutional documents such

as the faculty manual? Franke (2002) delineates a range of sanctions ranging from the termination of the offending faculty members to less harsh actions such as warning or reprimanding the individual, public censure, no salary increase or a reduction in salary, or requiring counseling or workshop attendance.

4. As previously specified in this chapter, our sample consisted of 100 liberal arts colleges: 38 public and 62 private institutions. Within this sample we found that 78 institutions—33 public institutions and 45 private institutions—promulgate institutional codes of conduct for undergraduate teaching that include at least one of the ten tenets delineated by Braxton and Bayer (2004). We recommend further research on these 78 institutions that also addresses the questions about the existence of integrity committees or sanctions for teaching misconduct.

We gain some degree of encouragement from our finding that the majority of four-year teaching-oriented colleges and universities represented in this study publicly display codes of conduct for undergraduate college teaching that include at least one of the ten tenets recommended by Braxton and Bayer (2004). Such codes protect the welfare of students as clients of undergraduate college teaching. However, if more of these tenets are included, the welfare of undergraduate students is more likely to be safeguarded. Fortunately, most of the institutions in our sample espouse more than one of the eleven tenets in their codes of conduct. The percentage distributions arrayed in Table 7.2 attest to this observation. Nevertheless, much work remains for both the communities of research and practice.

References

Braxton, J. M., and A. E. Bayer. 1999. *Faculty Misconduct in Collegiate Teaching*. Baltimore: Johns Hopkins University Press.

Braxton, J. M., and A. E. Bayer. 2004. "Toward a Code of Conduct for Undergraduate Teaching." In *Addressing Faculty and Student Classroom Improprieties*, New Directions for Teaching and Learning, no. 99, edited by J. M. Braxton and A. E. Bayer, 47–55. San Francisco: Jossey-Bass.

Braxton, J., A. Bayer, and J. Noseworthy. 2004. "The Influence of Teaching Norm Violations on the Welfare of Students as Clients of College Teaching." In *Addressing Faculty and Student Classroom Improprieties*, New Directions for Teaching and Learning, no. 99, edited by J. M. Braxton and A. E. Bayer, 41–46. San Francisco: Jossey-Bass.

Carnegie Foundation for the Advancement of Teaching. 2010. *The Carnegie Classification of Institutions of Higher Education*. Accessed September 12, 2010. http://classifications.carnegiefoundation.org/.

Colgate University. 2012. Faculty Handbook. http://www.colgate.edu/portaldata/imagegallerywww/87419dab-508f-4bc1-b6d1-c4580a90e02a/ImageGallery/Faculty Handbook Revisions for web 030211.pdf.

DiMaggio, P., and W. Powell. 1983. "The Iron Cage Revisited: Institutional Isomorphism and Collective Rationality in Organizational Fields." *American Sociological Review* 48: 147–160.

Franke, A. 2002, March 22. "Faculty Misconduct, Discipline, and Dismissal." Paper presented at the Annual Meeting of the National Association of College and University Attorneys, New Orleans, LA.

Zucker, L. G. 1987. "Institutional Theories of Organization." *Annual Review of Sociology* 13: 443–446.

Zuckerman, H. 1988. "The Sociology of Science." In *Handbook of Sociology,* edited by N. Smelser. Thousand Oaks, CA: Sage Publications.

DAWN LYKEN-SEGOSEBE *is a doctoral student in the Higher Education Leadership and Policy Studies program at Vanderbilt University. Previously, she lectured in the economics departments of the University of Guyana and the United Arab Emirates University and was a principal technical education officer in the Ministry of Education of Botswana.*

YUNKYUNG MIN *is a doctoral student in the Higher Education Leadership and Policy Studies program at Vanderbilt University.*

JOHN M. BRAXTON *is Professor of Education in the Higher Education Leadership and Policy Program at Peabody College of Vanderbilt University. Professor Braxton's scholarly interests include social control in academia with a particular focus on codes of conduct; norms; and the deterrence, detection, and sanctioning of violations of codes and norms.*

NEW DIRECTIONS FOR HIGHER EDUCATION • DOI:10.1002/he

8

This chapter addresses such topics as organizational principles underlying the development and functioning of codes, organizational constraints to the promulgation of codes, and organizational possibilities for the development of codes of conduct in higher education.

Organizational Constraints and Possibilities Regarding Codes of Conduct

Nathaniel J. Bray, Danielle K. Molina, Bart A. Swecker

Codes of ethics are the topic of this issue, and chapters explore aspects of their basic nature in the context of higher education. Fundamentally, ethical codes take on the most troublesome of behaviors related to academe and present ways for individuals to behave in the face of pressures and uncertainties. They represent the ideals of various stakeholder subgroups and even mediate key institutional relationships. Codes can also exist at different organizational levels in higher education, including professional association, institutional, and intra-institutional. Although they provide a stable set of ideals to which a given population can aspire, codes and their status appear to have changed over time. The existence of codes within and across diverse constituent groups suggests that the higher education community deems them both important and useful in the practices of university teaching, scholarship, and administration (Callahan 1982; Kerr 1994; Shurr 1982; Woody 2008). Still, we know relatively little about codes of ethics holistically or from a scholarly perspective.

Drawing upon research from higher education, specifically, and organizational studies more broadly, this chapter attempts to bring into focus a holistic view of higher education ethical codes from a scholarly perspective. The chapter reviews the rationale for ethical codes in a contemporary context of higher education and then provides an overview of the organizational principles underlying the development and functioning of the codes. We then look at the ways in which ethical codes have become organizational anchors for key constituent groups in higher education. Given these foundations for understanding the nature and evolution of ethical codes, the chapter concludes with a discussion of how codes of ethics are

NEW DIRECTIONS FOR HIGHER EDUCATION, no. 160, Winter 2012 © Wiley Periodicals, Inc.
Published online in Wiley Online Library (wileyonlinelibrary.com) • DOI:10.1002/he.20038

constrained in some ways by institutional structures and yet show promise for what they can offer.

The Rationale for Codes of Ethics in a Contemporary Context

Whether explicitly stated or implicitly practiced, codes of ethics shape the ways that individuals and groups within higher education view their roles. In turn, these worldviews affect nearly every important organizational process in higher education ranging from the teacher-student relationship to administrative decision-making. The chapters throughout this issue exemplify this range of organizational processes. Therefore, it is understandable that codes of ethics are challenged when behavior in higher education comes into question. In an era of increased scrutiny over higher education, the need for regulatory codes of ethics and conduct has become apparent (Bennett 1998). Moreover as this scrutiny continues, examination of codes and of the underlying expectations, norms, and behaviors will increase (Bennett 1998; Braxton and Bayer 1994; Reybold, Halx, and Jimenez 2008; Shurr 1982).

A complicating factor regarding ethical behavior in higher education is the fact that constituents often find themselves negotiating between expectations intersecting different levels of analysis. For instance, members of the academic community carry a unique responsibility to undertake teaching, research, and service to the campus and the public (American Association of University Professors 2012; Shurr 1982; Woody 2008). With this individual responsibility comes the need for a set of ideas that provide collective guidance for behaviors. However, standards cannot exist, or at least cannot be particularized, for every single behavior. As a result, both rules and codes of ethics tend to be proactive rather than prescriptive, just as they tend to focus on a more general, broadly applicable level rather than dealing with specifics.

Codes of ethics, then, seek to set a tone and more general guide for individuals. Kerr (1994, 11) states, "Any segment of society must have some common standards of conduct within it in order to operate effectively, different as these standards may be, including the intellectual." The need for unifying institutional codes of ethics is increasing as the landscape of questionable ethical choices and bad decisions continues (Bennett 1998; Braxton and Bayer 1994; Braxton, Proper, and Bayer 2011; Reybold, Halx, and Jimenez 2008; Shurr 1982). The establishment of a common code of ethics or a series of codes within the academy would provide the public assurance that employees of an institution would observe a set of rules and would provide those within the institution a standard of acceptable conduct and behavior (Bennett 1998).

Ethical Codes as Social Group Norms

Given the critical role that codes of ethics can play in shaping institutional behavior and the level of scrutiny likely to be placed upon these codes, it is helpful to understand what they inherently represent. One way to conceptualize codes of ethics is as sets of professional norms. The term "norm" refers to the informal and formal guidelines that exist to define what is accepted or inappropriate behavior within a social group (Merton 1968, 1973).

Norms often exist on a continuum, some demonstrating greater moral content than others. At the low end of the spectrum are social "folkways" or customs, whereas behaviors prompting a stronger response should they be violated are called "mores" (Macionis 2001). Whether they are customs or mores, norms can operate in either a positive and negative direction (Christensen, Rothgerber, Wood, and Matz 2004; Macionis 2001). For example, prescriptive (or injunctive) norms state what people should do. Meanwhile, proscriptive norms express what people should not do. Whereas prescriptive norms reinforce the values of a social group, proscriptive norms are often operationalized to protect a group's identity by sanctioning deviant behaviors in violation of group norms (Durkheim 1934; Erikson 1966).

Professional and Disciplinary Codes of Ethics in Higher Education

Although various sets of higher education constituents abide by ethical codes, social group norms have historically been devised for the purposes of shaping behavior within professions. A profession is defined as a self-regulating occupation that adheres to a common set of standards and training expectations (Braxton and Bayer 1994; Bruhn, Zajac, Al-Kazemi, and Prescott 2002; Wilson 1942). In colleges and universities professions may be delineated by student group, academic discipline, or administrative functional area.

Regardless of the unit, regulatory statements and standards provide a framework by which members of these communities can establish acceptable and responsible behaviors, seek to legitimize the profession, and address professional relationships (Bruhn et al. 2002; Callahan 1982). They also provide a roadmap of issues salient to the profession. For instance, ethical codes in academia often address four categories: (1) sexual harassment, (2) participants'/students' rights, (3) teaching students, and (4) research misconduct (Keith-Spiegel, Tabachnick, and Allen 1993).

Beyond setting expectations for behavior and delineating issues of importance to constituent groups, codes of ethics and conduct in higher education have been one method for establishing community in the faculty, staff, and students (Bruhn et al. 2002; Schurr 1982; Woody 2008). Kerr (1994, 11) states, "A well-accepted code of conduct is essential to any community of trust, and a community of trust is inherently more efficient than a community without trust." Although a universally accepted code of conduct is unlikely, many professional associations have achieved some measure of success among those within the organization.

NEW DIRECTIONS FOR HIGHER EDUCATION • DOI:10.1002/he

Association Codes. One set of bodies responsible for establishing professional expectations in the higher education community is professional associations (for example, the American Association of University Professors, the American Psychological Association, and the Modern Language Association). Rather than reflecting the values of individual colleges or universities, these associations are often specific to faculty discipline or administrative functional area. Principled in the values of professions, association codes sometimes come into conflict with institutional codes creating dissonance between key constituent groups (Kelley, Agle, and Demott 2006; Reybold, Halx, and Jimenez 2008). Therefore, some believe that association codes should drive institutional codes rather than the reverse (Kelley, Agle, and Demott 2006). Several examples follow.

Professional Associations for Faculty. In 1915, the American Association of University Professors (AAUP) released a statement on the principles of academic freedom and tenure. This document (in its original and 1925, 1940, 1970, and 1990 updated versions) outlined a guiding framework for professional educators, "to promote public understanding and support of academic freedom and tenure and agreement upon procedure to ensure them in colleges and universities" (AAUP 2012, para. 3). It was followed by a statement of professional ethics in 1966 (updated subsequently in 1987 and 2009) (AAUP 2012). Ultimately, the goal of the AAUP document is to offer a group of standards that spans disciplines and institutional types, while leaving the responsibility for addressing specific ethical situations, regulating behavior, and enforcing codes to individual institutions (AAUP 2012; Bruhn et al. 2002; Strom-Gottfried and D'Aprix 2006). Such an approach increases the need for institutions to develop enforceable codes that work in conjunction with those found in professional associations (Bennett 1998; Bruhn et al. 2002).

Professional Associations for Higher Education Research and Practice. The Association for the Study of Higher Education's (ASHE) released the "ASHE Principles of Ethical Conduct" in 2003. This code includes a set of ten areas for behavioral concern, including integrity, credit, responsibility, honesty and accuracy, originality, respect, fairness, advancement, responsibility to clients and to the public interest, and finally conflict of interest. These ten areas indicate key areas of concern for those within the profession, highlighting their importance in addition to providing ideas for behavior. The American Educational Research Association (AERA), on the other hand, has had a set of Ethical Standards since 1992, updated in 2011 to a Code of Ethics. Although much of the code specifically addresses research behavior, the report includes commentary around twenty-two ethical standards and has specific commentary on areas such as harassment, mentoring, public communications, and contracting services. Meanwhile, the American Association of University Administrators (AAUA 1994) offers a list of eighteen behaviors with paired sets of rights and responsibilities for administrators in each of the resulting areas.

NEW DIRECTIONS FOR HIGHER EDUCATION • DOI:10.1002/he

Professional Associations for Disciplines. The Modern Language Association (MLA) adopted a professional code of ethics in 1991 and most recently revised this document in 2004 (Modern Language Association 2012). The MLA code seeks to address conduct in teaching, learning, scholarship, and service for the teachers and scholars comprising its membership (MLA 2012, n.p.). The MLA code notes, "A common understanding of such obligations will enable us to exert appropriate restraints in exercising our responsibilities as scholars, teachers, and students and to promote ethical behavior in our departments and institutions."

The American Psychological Association's (APA) code of ethics addresses professional areas of competence, confidentiality, and conflicts of interests (American Psychological Association 2012). The APA notes that a code of ethics works in possible conjunction with other regulatory guidelines, and where the code of ethics requires a higher standard than the law, the higher standard must be met (APA 2012). This code seeks to provide guidance to individual psychologists engaged in research, teaching, or their professional role as a psychologist (APA 2012). Schurr (1982) notes that enforcement of a code of ethics is an important factor to consider during code development. Many associations' codes lack the necessary ability to enforce, and often do not outline sanctions for violations (Bennett 1998). The APA, however, does provide regulatory statements through its code of ethics and outlines possible sanctions that may arise due to a violation of the code (APA 2012).

Isomorphic Pressures and the Migration toward Normative Codes of Ethics

Whether codes exist to serve professions, institutions, or both simultaneously, any set of standards must pass through the filter of individual constituents before it is accepted, carried out, or enforced. In other words, group norms are only meaningful if individual constituents adopt them. However, each person interprets reality individually. Therefore, discrepancies occasionally arise between individual schemas for behavioral norms and disciplinary or institutional directives (Erikson 1966). Given that situation, only widely held values may be placed in a code of ethics. This can cause a form of isomorphism in which norms become codified, and institutions eventually trend toward the adoption of similar codes (Lyken-Segosebe, Min, and Braxton, chapter 7).

Isomorphism around ethical codes in higher education occurs when attempts to frame unique expectations for a particular social group migrate toward similar organizational language, practices, and/or structures at a field level. As Lyken-Segosebe, Min, and Braxton argue earlier in this issue, ethical codes can be a sign of isomorphic pressures for either normative or mimetic behavior on the part of groups, departments, professions, or institutions. In normative responses to isomorphic pressures, groups adopt language, practices, and organizational structures that appear legitimate in the eyes of their peers. In mimetic responses, institutions deliberately replicate what other institutions are doing. In either case, the result is a trend toward campus codes that share the same basic content.

A question can be raised, then, as to whether ethical codes accomplish their goal to authentically reflect the values of, and provide guidelines for, their individual organizations (Forster, Loughran, and McDonald 2009; Long and Driscoll 2008). Colleges and universities are situated in an environmental context of competition, fast-paced changed, and calls from external forces for accountability. Given the pressures facing institutions and this isomorphic tendency in codes, there are several possibilities for overall work with codes of ethics in higher education and larger shared values. However, as with many things, strength can also be a weakness, and the very positives that codes have to offer may come with constraints as well.

Constraints and Possibilities

Because codes speak to group expectations, they represent unique ways of looking at group values, constraints, and flexibility for growth, movement, and change. However, there are challenges to their use, just as there are possibilities to improve the way they have been used.

Constraints. From a functionalist perspective, a social system is comprised of, nurtured through, and sustained by an interrelated set of component parts. Although these components collectively contribute to the stability of the parent system, each component also serves a specific purpose to achieve such an outcome (Donaldson 2005). Throughout this chapter, we have recognized several ways in which ethical codes enhance the vitality of higher education, including regulating behavior, rewarding obedience, coalescing constituents around common values, and establishing legitimacy among peer organizations. Given such benefits, it is easy to understand why administrative leaders, professional organizations, and academic disciplines take extensive measures to create such codes as guides to higher education practice.

Still, codes of ethics do not come without their problems. They often take considerable time and effort to devise, only to ultimately meet scrutiny as to their meaning and utility (Morphew and Hartley 2006). Moreover in any organizational context, higher education or otherwise, constraints potentially limit the ways in which codes are created, implemented, and used by both internal and external constituents. Such universal challenges highlight the obstacles that can be encountered in related higher education efforts.

One organizational constraint on ethical codes in higher education involves the nature of encoding values intended to be representative across diverse organizational terrain. Like mission statements, codes of ethics are guidelines that depict values and practices within a discipline, a department, or an institution. However, beyond the fact that there are different levels of organization operating simultaneously in higher education, each of these levels involve complex relationships between constituents, conflicting tensions between the values of these constituents, and divergent aspirational outcomes. Owing to such complexities, penning a code of ethics can be an overwhelming and seemingly unrealistic task (Callahan 1982; Schurr 1982). Moreover, if a code of ethics can be achieved, it is likely to be more symbolic than practically useful (Callahan 1982). Therefore questions arise as to whether the energy expended in framing such codes is worth its rigor. More specifically, universities may devote a great deal of effort into creating codes of ethics only to find that either the guidelines are not being followed or they are difficult to enforce.

A second constraint, then, revolves around the question of what an ethical code actually symbolizes if it is not the real values and useful guidelines of a college or university. At the level of a college or university, value statements, like codes of ethics or mission statements, have a dual intent. On the one hand, they are intended to inform the public as to the institution's identity. On the other hand, value statements are designed to guide internal institutional practices. These two goals are often at odds, leaving value statements that represent images of an institution as it would like to be seen rather than how the institution actually operates (Morphew and Hartley 2006). Such a discrepancy creates a situation where there are often two sets of values at work in a college or university at the same time: explicit values represented by the code of ethics and implicit values espoused by the daily practices at an institution (Astin 1989).

A third constraint involves the aforementioned variegated landscape of stakeholder groups and subgroups. The more widely diversified the groups are, the more differentiation there is between implicit values and a shared set of explicit values espoused in a code. This brings to the foreground power differentials that exist between traditionally empowered and disempowered constituents in higher education. For instance, majority groups (often Caucasian and male administrators or faculty) or powerful actors across academic disciplines (for example, faculty in science, technology, engineering, and mathematics) currently may have larger suasion in defining the code of ethical behaviors than those from historically marginalized social identity or academic groups. (Alpert 1985; Gumport 2000). In another example, inconsistencies between the explicit values set out in the ethical code and the implicit values practiced within an institution can create conflict among and between faculty and administration. Resulting feelings of tension, disillusionment, isolation, resentment, and even anger can undermine the original purpose of an ethical statement in the first place: unity around shared values.

At the disciplinary level, codes of ethics also take on symbolic importance in that they are purported to distinguish one institution's values and behavioral expectations from another. Yet, as discussed, higher education faces ethical imperatives and environmental challenges that place isomorphic pressures on articulating related values statements (Couch and Dodd 2005; Morphew and Hartley 2006; Taylor and Morphew 2010; Weegar 2007), such as rising competition, globalization, fast-paced environmental change, and calls from external forces for accountability (Bloland 2005; Currie 2003; Eckel 2006; Tierney and Rhoades 1993; Wellford and Zell 2003). Consequently, it is difficult to develop ethical guidelines that are simultaneously meaningful at the institutional level in higher education and legitimate in the eyes of various external stakeholders (for example, professional organizations, accreditation bodies, government agencies, society at large). Moreover, ethical guidelines developed in the wake of isomorphic pressures tell outsiders little about a particular organization and provide insiders few guidelines on how to shape their practices (Chua and Rahman 2011; Forster, Loughran, and McDonald 2009; Long and Driscoll 2008). As a result, codes tend to be responsive more than proactive, which limits their utility in helping reduce confusion about how to handle new situations.

A final constraint revolves around the effectiveness of ethical codes in light of organizational culture and climate. Once an institution, department, or professional organization has achieved an actual ethical code, higher education constituents may feel that they have attained their goal of creating a values-centered organization. However, research shows that unethical behavior often persists in spite of the fact that an ethical code exists (VanSandt and Neck 2003). Organizational culture and climate play important roles in mediating this discrepancy (Sims 1991; Stevens 2008; Verbos et al. 2007). Particularly, ethical codes do little to affect organizational climate unless leaders and managers perceive the guidelines to be useful (Wotruba, Chonko, and Loe 2001) and embody related values in their actions (Andreoli and Lefkowitz 2009; Stevens 2008; Watson 2003). In fact, due to the nature of their work, educators may be best served by foregrounding their own personal evolution of ethical values over those espoused in an ethical code (Niesche and Haase 2010). Therefore, unless top ranking faculty and administrators opt to exemplify ethical behavior, the act of encoding ethical rules may turn out to be perfunctory rather than meaningful. Furthermore, unless those in higher education are allowed to explore their personal connections to ethical values, they may find themselves disconnected from the formalized goals of an ethical code altogether.

Possibilities. Given the range of constraints related to creating, implementing, and enforcing codes of ethics within higher education contexts, one may question whether these statements are worth the time and effort they demand (Morphew and Hartley 2006). The good news is that, despite their challenges, codes of ethics can be effective in mediating unethical behavior in higher education (Rezaee, Elmore, and Szendi 2001) and thus are rife with possibility for infusing shared values into college and university dynamics. Understanding ethical lapses in higher education and the path necessary to correct them is an important step in producing better ethical behavior (Kelley and Chang 2007). Institutional and professional codes of ethics provide the framework from which to judge many of the decisions of those who work and study in colleges and universities. A code of ethics that is enforceable and allows for easily understanding correct behavior (Kelley, Agle, and Demott 2006; Reybold, Halx, and Jimenez 2008) can ultimately instill the idea of proper ethical behavior and developing trust among colleagues in higher education (Kelley and Chang 2007).

Conversely, the enforcement of ethical codes has brought to the surface previously hidden ethical lapses, especially regarding fiscal and classroom matters (Bennett 1998; Kerr 1994; Rezaee, Elmore, and Szendi 2001; Somers 2001). Showing an effort toward concern and due diligence around such matters builds public trust between higher education and the public at large, a challenge continually faced in our profession (Rezaee, Elmore, and Szendi 2001). Codes may offer that, and a number of studies have found a positive outlook for codes of conduct within the academy (for example, Bruhn et al. 2002; Kerr 1994; Rezaee et al. 2001; Schurr 1982; Woody 2008). Callahan (1982) states that codes of ethics serve to establish a set of commonly held rules and develop a definition of the profession. Schurr (1982) outlines the necessary topics that must be considered in a professional code of ethics: (1) auditability, (2) service to society, (3) avoiding conflicts of interest, (4) efficacy of instruction, (5) reliable evaluation, (6) differentiation among specializations, (7) certification of professional competence, (8) relationship among specializations, (9) specificity in elaboration, and (10) enforcement. A few of the most critical and central of these are explored in more detail next.

Service to society is central to the mission of academia. Development of a code of ethics can help to demonstrate the applicability of higher education to the larger society, thereby instilling value (Shurr 1982; Woody 2008). Codes of ethics are products of the society and culture in which they exist and may only reflect the ideas that make them relevant to their individual culture (Reybold, Halx, and Jimenez 2008). Remaining relevant to a broader culture and evaluating a profession's contribution to society are central to protect the group that a code serves. With the outside culture continuing to display distrust for higher education, the need to express worth and service to society is necessary (Bruhn et al. 2002). This is particularly important in the areas that are most visible to society, especially those related to the core areas of teaching and research.

Competence of teaching and research should work to appropriately combine personal ethics in order to introduce excellence in the classroom and openly identify bias and conflicts of interest (Bruhn et al. 2002; Shurr 1982; Woody 2008). Codes in higher education often emphasize the areas of knowledge dissemination and generation, training of future professionals, and suitable behavior when handling students' data and treatment

(MLA 2012; Woody 2008). Avoiding conflicts of interest, having proper efficacy in instruction, and establishing reliable evaluation are essential to teaching in higher education (Bruhn et al. 2002; Shurr 1982). However, higher education faculty and staff often do not leave their personal belief structure behind when they begin to work at an institution (Reybold, Halx, and Jimenez 2008), so efforts to protect against bias take on a critical need for a clearly stated code of ethics.

Given the importance of these areas, auditability is an essential part of any code that seeks to define the desirable and expected outcomes of the behaviors as defined by a code of ethics (Hatcher 2011; Shurr 1982). Hatcher (2011) notes that codes of ethics often have two types of behaviors: advocated ethics—those behaviors that are endorsed, and performed ethics—those behaviors that are allowed. Advocated ethics are those that should be outlined in a code, and performed ethics should be those behaviors that are managed by the enforcement side of the codes (Hatcher 2011). Bennett (1998, 89) states that disciplinary codes "risk being hortatory artifacts" without proper enforcement methods. Along with auditability is also the idea of enforcement (Schurr 1982); for codes to be most effective, there needs to be a way for sanctioning undesirable behavior. Auditability is an area where associations with certification processes often outpace institutions. The effort to improve both auditability and enforcement within institutions is hampered by increasing levels of differentiation in the academy.

Specialization of disciplines and fields of study make the codes of professional associations even more important. Specialization within administrative roles also occurs, as evidenced in the chapters by Fleming, Bray, Caboni, and Hodum in this issue. With the constraint of such fragmentation and likely increased difficulties in finding solid comprehensive grounds for a code across the entire campus, the possibility exists for a rise in the importance of disciplinary codes, particularly among professional associations. Professional organizations (for example, American Bar Association, American Medical Association, Certified Financial Planners) have, as part of their certification process, a core code of ethical conduct that members of the organization agree to uphold and to accept consequences when violations occur (Bennett 1998; Bruhn et al. 2002; Kelley, Agle, and Demott 2006; Reybold, Halx, and Jimenez 2008). Professional associations in the law and medical professions often have the ability to sanction members for misconduct (Strom-Gottfried and D'Aprix 2006), for example. Thus, higher education institutions should explore the idea of ethical certification processes, if only to be able to better address violations of codes of ethics in a professional and informational manner (Bennett 1998; Braxton and Bayer 1994; Kerr 1994).

As noted previously, as the level of specialization in higher education grows, the need for better responses to differentiation and for building relationships between disciplines through stated codes has increased as well (Shurr 1982; Bennett 1998). Disciplines are becoming split by their methodological approach and the ideologies of the profession, creating further separation from a standard code of acceptable behaviors and ethics (Kerr 1994). This provides opportunities for disciplinary codes, as noted previously. Yet, it also provides the opportunity for institutional stakeholders to engage in a soul-searching process about what their institution stands for and how things are meant to be. This may in part help counteract some of the effects of fragmentation as well, for a unifying code must depart from, as Bennett (1998, 91) states, "departments [which] promote specialization and separation rather than breadth and unity of inquiry." Institutions can quickly become silos of departments, groups of students, and disciplines, all with varying ideas regarding ethical conduct (Bennett 1998; Reybold, Halx, and Jimenez 2008).

Thus, differentiation of and relationship among specializations can, if done correctly, help lead to a central behavior code that serves the campus community and the disciplinary differences jointly (Bennett 1998; Shurr 1982). For example, when constituents at different levels of an organization are invited into the process of creating an ethical code, it inspires these individuals to engage in work consistent with the values contained therein (Gilley, Robertson, and Mazur 2010). This involvement strategy can have long-term effects on the organization by allowing individuals at different levels of higher education the opportunity to take ownership of its values and to imagine ways of carrying on the legacy in their own work. Alternatively, it may not even take such concerted involvement efforts to engage students, faculty, administrators, and staff in a values-centered mindset. The mere existence of an ethical code can have a positive impact by shaping the perception and behavior of organizational constituents (Adams, Tashchian, and Shore 2001). Therefore, leaders framing a code of ethics may prioritize getting a workable statement into place over spending inordinate time and resources to perfect it.

Enforcement, as discussed before, is difficult with codes of ethics (Kelley, Agle, and Demott 2006; Reybold, Halx, and Jimenez 2008). Associations with certification processes are often the small group that has a path of recourse should principles be violated. Institutions have a set of expectations for employees regarding work expectations, but this may not extend to ethical situations. Certification of central competencies and understanding of a standard set of expected behaviors could increase the ability to enforce standards and promote the applicability of higher education to the larger society (Callahan 1982; Shurr 1982; Woody 2008).

Whether a code of ethics has been internalized actively or passively, putting these perceptions into practice via role modeling ethically consistent behavior has more than a small impact on perpetuating a values-centered organizational culture and climate (Grojean et al. 2004; Verbos et al. 2007; Watson 2003). Therefore, resources to support ethically consistent behavior could yield significant returns. One approach might include improving new employee orientations or other forms of socialization to help constituents better understand the explicit ethical expectations within their areas and to envision means of carrying out these expectations in their daily practice. Another approach might include an in-service activity where constituents within a particular group can discuss and possibly amend discrepancies between explicit expectations and implicit practices. A final approach might include formalizing a program to recognize and reinforce practices that exemplify the ethical code.

Conclusion

In response to scrutiny over higher education practices and corresponding calls for accountability, colleges and universities have adopted codes of ethics as a means for regulating behavior. A code of ethics is a values-centered set of collective norms that formalizes expectations for academic disciplines, departments, professional organizations, or institutions at large. It is intended to signal appropriate behavior to the public at the same time it serves as a self-regulating mechanism within each of these areas. However, codes of ethics can also be envisioned as means of bridging relationships between constituents traditionally separated into silos such as groups of students, departments, and academic specializations.

Although theoretically sound in concept, codes of ethics are constrained by some of the same institutional and field-level dynamics encountered in any set of organizations subscribing to this strategy. For instance, because ethical codes must simultaneously represent specific expectations and generalizable rules for a constituent group, codes are difficult to devise, often ambiguous with regards to practical application, and challenging to enforce. Therefore, they become symbolic statements rather than the guiding principles originally intended. Discrepancies between these symbolic explicit codes outlined in formal documents and the implicit codes actually practiced within institutions can cause conflicts among and between students, faculty, and administrators. Further, normative language used to frame ethical codes often renders them symbols of isomorphic legitimacy rather than statements of distinctive organizational expectations. Finally, formalized codes of ethics have little effect on enhancing organizational climate or culture if not explored on a personalized basis and role modeled by organizational leaders.

Conversely, and perhaps outweighing some of their common pitfalls, there is an inherent promise in the idea of ethical codes for enhancing the culture and climate of higher education departments, disciplines, and institutions. For example, although the actual content of an ethical code might be debatable, the existence of that code can positively influence the perceptions and actions of constituents such that these contribute to a corresponding values-centered organizational climate and culture. Whether through involvement or via diffusion, individuals who internalize ethical codes and model consistent behavior in their daily practices can also contribute to an enhanced organizational climate and culture. Therefore, resources should be allocated to support constituents in reaching this goal through formalized education, dialogue, and recognition opportunities.

References

Adams, J. S., A. Tashchian, and T. H. Shore. 2001. "Codes of Ethics as Signals for Ethical Behavior." *Journal of Business Ethics* 29(3): 199–211.

Alpert, D. 1985. "Performance and Paralysis: The Organizational Context of the American Research University." *Journal of Higher Education* 56(3): 241–281.

American Association of University Administrators. 1994. *A.A.U.A. Statement of Professional Standards for Adminstrators in Higher Education.* http://www.aaua.org/aboutus/aboutus.htm.

American Association of University Professors. 2012. *Policy Documents and Reports Website.* http://www.aaup.org/AAUP/pubsres/policydocs.

American Educational Research Association. 2011. *Code of Ethics.* http://www.aera.net/Portals/38/docs/About_AERA/CodeOfEthics(1).pdf.

American Psychological Association. 2012. *Ethical Principles of Psychologists and Code of Conduct.* http://www.apa.org/ethics/code/.

Andreoli, N., and J. Lefkowitz. 2009. "Individual and Organizational Antecedents of Misconduct in Organizations." *Journal of Business Ethics* 85: 309–332.

Association for the Study of Higher Education. 2003. *ASHE Principles of Ethical Conduct.* http://www.ashe.ws/?page=180.

Astin, A. 1989. "Moral Messages of the University." *Educational Record* 70(1): 22–25.

Bennett, J. 1998. *Collegial Professionalism: The Academy, Individualism, and the Common Good.* Phoenix: Oryx Press.

Bloland, H. G. 2005. "Whatever Happened to Postmodernism in Higher Education? No Requiem in the New Millennium." *Journal of Higher Education* 76(2): 121–150.

Braxton, J. M., and A. E. Bayer. 1994. "Perceptions of Research Misconduct and an Analysis of Their Correlates." *Journal of Higher Education* 65(3): 351–372.

Braxton, J. M., E. Proper, and A. E. Bayer. 2011. *Professors Behaving Badly: Faculty Misconduct in Graduate Education.* Baltimore: Johns Hopkins University Press.

Bruhn, J., G. Zajac, A. Al-Kazemi, and L. Prescott. 2002. "Moral Positions and Academic Conduct: Parameters of Tolerance for Ethics Failure." *Journal of Higher Education* 73(4): 461–493.

Callahan, D. 1982. "Should There Be an Academic Code of Ethics?" *Journal of Higher Education* 53(3): 335–344.

Christensen, P. N., H. Rothgerber, W. Wood, and D. C. Matz. 2004. "Social Norms and Identity Relevance: A Motivational Approach to Normative Behavior." *Personality and Social Psychology Bulletin* 30: 1295–1309.

Chua, F., and A. Rahman. 2011. "Institutional Pressures and Ethical Reckoning by Business Corporations." *Journal of Business Ethics* 98: 307–329.

Couch, S., and S. Dodd. 2005. "Doing the Right Thing: Ethical Issues in Higher Education." *Journal of Family and Consumer Sciences* 97(3): 20–26.

Currie, J. 2003. "Globalization and Universities." In *Higher Education: A Handbook of Theory and Research,* Vol. 18, edited by W. Tierney, 473–530. Dordrecht, The Netherlands: Kluwer Press.

Donaldson, L. 2005. "Organization Theory as a Positive Science." In *The Oxford Handbook of Organization: Meta-Theoretical Perspectives,* edited by H. Tsoukas and C. Knudsen. Oxford, UK: Oxford University Press.

Durkheim, E. 1934. *The Elementary Focus of Religious Life.* London: Allen & Unwin. (Original manuscript written 1912).

Eckel, P. D. 2006. *The Shifting Frontiers of Academic Decision Making: Responding to New Priorities, Following New Pathways.* Westport, CT: Praeger.

Erikson, K. T. 1966. *Wayward Puritans: A Study in the Sociology of Deviance.* New York: MacMillan.

Forster, M., T. Loughran, and B. McDonald. 2009. "Commonality in Codes of Ethics." *Journal of Business Ethics* 90: 129–139.

Gilley, K. M., C. J. Robertson, and T. C. Mazur. 2010. "The Bottom-Line Benefits of Ethics Code Commitment." *Business Horizons* 53(1): 31–37.

Grojean, M. W., C. J. Resick, M. W. Dickson, and D. B. Smith. 2004. "Leaders, Values, and Organizational Climate: Examining Leadership Strategies for Establishing an Organizational Climate Regarding Ethics." *Journal of Business Ethics* 55: 223–241.

Gumport, P. J. 2000. "Academic Restructuring: Organizational Change and Institutional Imperatives." *Higher Education* 39: 67–91.

Hatcher, T. 2011. "Becoming an Ethical Scholarly Writer." *Journal of Scholarly Publishing* 42(2): 142–159.

Keith-Spiegel, P., B. Tabachnick, and M. Allen. 1993. "Ethics in Academia: Students' Views of Professors' Actions." *Ethics and Behavior* 3(2): 149–162.

Kelley, P., and P. Chang. 2007. "A Typology of University Ethical Lapses: Types, Levels of Seriousness, and Originating Location." *Journal of Higher Education* 78(4): 402–429.

Kelley, P., B. Agle, and J. Demott. 2006. "Mapping Our Progress: Identifying, Categorizing and Comparing Universities' Ethics Infrastructures." *Journal of Academic Ethics* 3: 205–229.

Kerr, C. 1994. "Knowledge Ethics and the New Academic Culture." *Change* 26(1): 8–15.

Long, B. S., and C. Driscoll. 2008. "Codes of Ethics and the Pursuit of Organizational Legitimacy: Theoretical and Empirical Contributions." *Journal of Business Ethics* 77: 173–189.

Macionis, J. J. 2001. *Sociology,* 8th ed. Upper Saddle River, NJ: Prentice Hall.

Merton, R. K. 1968. *Social Science and Social Structure.* New York: Free Press.

Merton, R. K. 1973. *The Sociology of Science: Theoretical and Empirical Investigations.* Chicago: University of Chicago Press.

Modern Language Association. 2012. *Statement of Professional Ethics.* http://www.mla.org/repview_profethics.

Morphew, C. C., and M. Hartley. 2006. "A Thematic Analysis of Rhetoric Across Institutional Type." *Journal of Higher Education* 77(3): 456–471.

Niesche, R., and M. Haase. 2010. "Emotions and Ethics: A Foucauldian Framework for Becoming an Ethical Educator." *Educational Philosophy and Theory* 44(3): 276–288.

Reybold, L., M. Halx, and A. Jimenez. 2008. "Professional Integrity in Higher Education: A Study of Administrative Staff Ethics in Student Affairs." *Journal of College Student Development* 49(2): 110–124.

Rezaee, Z., R. C. Elmore, and J. Z. Szendi. 2001. "Ethical Behavior in Higher Educational Institutions: The Role of the Code of Conduct." *Journal of Business Ethics* 30: 171–183.

Shurr, G. 1982. "Toward a Code of Ethics for Academics." *Journal of Higher Education* 53(3): 318–334.

Sims, R. R. 1991. "The Institutionalization of Organizational Ethics." *Journal of Business Ethics* 10: 493–506.

Somers, J. 2001. "Ethical Codes of Conduct and Organizational Context: A Study of the Relationship between Codes of Conduct, Employee Behavior and Organizational Values." *Journal of Business Ethics* 30: 185–195.

Stevens, B. 2008. "Corporate Ethical Codes: Effective Instruments for Influencing Behavior." *Journal of Business Ethics* 78: 601–609.

Strom-Gottfried, K., and A. D'Aprix. 2006. "Ethics for Academics." *Social Work Education* 25(3): 225–244.

Taylor, B. J., and C. C. Morphew. 2010. "An Analysis of Baccalaureate College Mission Statements." *Research in Higher Education* 51: 483–503.

Tierney, W. G., and R. A. Rhoades. 1993. "Postmodernism and Critical Theory in Higher Education: Implications for Research and Practice." In *Higher Education: Handbook of Theory and Research*, Vol. 9, edited by J. C. Smart, 308–343. New York: Agathon Press.

VanSandt, C. V., and C. P. Neck. 2003. "Bridging Ethics and Self Leadership: Overcoming Discrepancies between Employee and Organizational Standards." *Journal of Business Ethics* 43: 363–387.

Verbos, A. K., J. A. Gerard, P. R. Forshey, C. S. Harding, and J. S. Miller. 2007. "The Positive Ethical Organization: Enacting a Living Code of Ethics and Ethical Organizational Identity." *Journal of Business Ethics* 76: 17–33.

Watson, T. J. 2003. "Ethical Choice in Managerial Work: The Scope for Moral Choices in an Ethically Irrational World." *Human Relations* 56(2): 167–185.

Weegar, M. A. 2007. "Promoting Ethical Practices within Institutions of Higher Education." Proceedings from the Association for Business Communication Annual Convention, October 10–12, Washington, DC.

Wellford, W. W., and D. M. Zell. 2003. "Accelerating Change in the Academy: Balancing New Demands While Protecting Core Values." *On the Horizon* 11(3): 16–22.

Wilson, L. 1942. *The Academic Man: A Study in Sociology of a Profession*. New York: Oxford University Press.

Woody, W. 2008. "Learning from the Codes of the Academic Disciplines." In *Practical Approaches to Ethics for Colleges and Universities*, New Directions for Higher Education, no. 142, edited by S. L. Moore, 39–54. San Francisco: Jossey-Bass.

Wotruba, T. R., L. B. Chonko, and T. W. Loe. 2001. "The Impact of Ethics Code Familiarity on Manager Behavior." *Journal of Business Ethics* 33: 59–69.

NATHANIEL J. BRAY *is an associate professor and program coordinator in Higher Education Administration at the University of Alabama. His research interests include normative structures for academic administrators, sociology of higher education, and student issues across higher education.*

DANIELLE K. MOLINA *is a clinical assistant professor in Higher Education Administration at the University of Alabama.*

BART A. SWECKER *is a Ph.D. candidate in higher education administration at the University of Alabama and assistant director of enrollment management communications at the University of Alabama at Birmingham.*

NEW DIRECTIONS FOR HIGHER EDUCATION • DOI:10.1002/he

9

*This chapter discusses asymmetries that exist in both
positional and professional authority, the relations between
main campus stakeholders, and the vulnerabilities that are
presented by such power differentials. The chapter concludes
with a discussion of the deterrence, detection, and sanctioning
of violations of tenets of codes of conduct.*

Reflections on Codes of Conduct: Asymmetries, Vulnerabilities, and Institutional Controls

Nathaniel J. Bray, John M. Braxton

Codes of conduct can and should fulfill a critical role in higher education. Codes help overcome some of the challenges inherent in a system predicated on high levels of autonomy (Braxton and Bayer 1999) and on self-regulation (Volkwein 1999; Zusman 2005). Codes not only are important indicators of critical topics that are deemed worthy of explicit protection or expectations for behavior; they may often protect those in positions of vulnerability or asymmetry.

Given profound institutional powers and the too often subsequent failures of institutional checks and balances and reporting functions (see for example Freeh, Sporkin, and Sullivan, LLC 2012), higher education continues to be at a critical juncture in considering how best to handle self-regulation. Over the past two decades, codes have continued to be revised and developed (see American Educational Research Association 2011), although too slowly. Given the difficulty in defining codes across the system or even an institution of higher education (see Vaughan 1992), the comments from Kerr (1972, 1986) that suggest institutional differentiation is fracturing into "dissensus" and that governance quality is actually dropping make the consideration of the topic one that should be revisited regularly. To this end, the focus of this work is on the nature of institutional asymmetries and vulnerabilities as well as the sanctioning, detection, and deterrence of the behaviors listed in empirically derived codes of conduct.

NEW DIRECTIONS FOR HIGHER EDUCATION, no. 160, Winter 2012   © Wiley Periodicals, Inc.
Published online in Wiley Online Library (wileyonlinelibrary.com) • DOI:10.1002/he.20039

Current Empirical Understanding of Codes of Conduct

As we have seen from the work of Braxton and Bayer (1999) and the chapters in this issue by Bray; Caboni; Fleming; Hodum; Lyken-Segosebe, Min, and Braxton; and Proper (2012), codes exist currently at various levels, from professional associations to institutions. The aforementioned authors posit specific, empirically based codes of conduct for levels across colleges and universities, from several levels and specific areas of administrative functioning to guidelines for faculty dealing primarily with graduate or undergraduate students.

There are inherent challenges in trying to formulate empirically based codes. First, empirical testing must be derived from the often-discordant literature. There may be little empirical work guiding the efforts of leading authors to comb through the guidelines of the American Association of University Administrators (AAUA), American Association of University Professors (AAUP), or other group or individual directives or expostulations as a baseline to begin empirical testing. Furthermore, constituent groups or stakeholders may vary enough to make codification of expectations for behavior difficult. Third, such an effort at codification must move beyond moral platitudes or good behaviors that any person should consider, but instead manage to get at the heart of the specific position being considered. Administrators, for example, should not be exhorted to be visionaries or intellectually curious. These are standard behavioral expectations. Instead, codes should have specific postulations for precisely how administrators should perform their roles.

As the authors noted previously have indicated, work on codes for presidents, deans, admissions officers, advancement officers, and graduate as well as undergraduate faculty finds that there are some commonalities that can perhaps combat some of the dissensus noted by Kerr (1972). These commonalities show some central values that are considered important across academe, even though their embodiment differs based on the position for which the code of conduct is being forwarded.

Bray (2008) also notes the importance not only of the group in question-defining, self-policing, and sanctioning behavior but also the central role of faculty in policing the institution, particularly vis-à-vis the role of the academic dean. Given the findings of Freeh, Sporkin, and Sullivan (2012) on the recent issues at Penn State, it should be abundantly clear the role all institutional members play in identifying and taking corrective action when coming into contact with inappropriate behavior. More than ever, developing clearer and stronger codes of conduct, codes that identify inappropriate behavior and clarify steps to take no matter the campus power differentials, is a central need in higher education. In that sense, many of the codes espoused by the authors presented above could be developed further.

To alleviate the issue of dissensus (Kerr 1972), though, there are several tenets that resonated across stakeholder groups. The first and most prevalent of these was the topic of communication, which is a central component to many of the empirically based codes (see the chapters by Bray; Caboni; Fleming; Hodum; and Lyken-Segosebe et al.). This is not surprising given the literature robust with discussion of silos and ivory towers, of cosmopolitan versus local foci, and other issues. Open communication is in fact a central element of Freeh, Sporkin, and Sullivan (2012) for steps to take in moving forward to improve the institutional culture and ethical functioning at Penn State. Each of the empirically derived codes that mention communication points to the need for timely and effective communication that shares with essential stakeholders information needed to move the institution forward with effective governance. Campus groups may have different expectations of what this looks like, but given its importance, dialogue around communication and expectations for timelines and effectiveness should be pursued.

Codes of conduct consistently reflect an expectation of morality, several noting the inappropriateness of any kind of sexual behavior across stakeholder groups, either in the tenets of the codes themselves or in the norms that underlie them (Bray 2008; Fleming, chapter 2; Lyken-Segosebe et al., chapter 7). If not specifically noting the inappropriateness of sexual interactions with any stakeholders, other codes note the need for moral behavior by indicating not taking advantage of those individuals who do not have full control of their faculties (Caboni, chapter 5) and embodying honesty and integrity (Hodum, chapter 4).

Use of institutional resources also is seen as a point of consensus across codes of conduct. Fleming's findings in chapter 2 point to presidents' acquisition of resources, Bray's findings in chapter 3 note deans' need to be sound fiscal managers following budgetary agreements, and Caboni's findings in chapter 5 indicate that fund-raisers should use resources in a frugal manner.

Both of the empirically derived codes for faculty behavior indicate the importance of respect and mentorship of students. Tenets include being fair (Proper, chapter 6) and respecting confidentiality of students (Lyken-Segosebe et al., chapter 7). Student access and faculty availability are also a central area of concern.

A key component of many of the themes seen across the codes of conduct for various administrator and faculty positions is the asymmetry that can exist in relationships on campus, as well as the vulnerabilities produced by these asymmetries. These vulnerabilities often are the focus of the protection through the tenets of the codes of conduct. The discussion of institutional asymmetries and associated vulnerabilities forms the crux of the following section.

Asymmetries and Vulnerabilities

As Bray, Molina, and Swecker note in chapter 8, the interstices of the levels of higher education, between faculty and students, between administrators and faculty, or even differing layers of administration, can lead to issues that prompt codes of conduct. These connective points between layers are ultimately where many power differentials lie as well as vulnerabilities that require extra protections be set in place. Asymmetries are lacks of proportion or lacks of balance in spatial relations. In higher education, asymmetries can be those of formal or positional authority such as between levels of administrators or between administrators and faculty. There are also asymmetries based upon imbalances of professional authority or expertise, which may arise between senior and junior faculty for instance.

Codes of conduct often are aimed at protecting those who cannot protect themselves or are at a power differential. This section highlights both the major asymmetries in the system, focusing first on those asymmetries caused by differences in positional authority and then those caused by differences in professional authority, and also the vulnerabilities for each major asymmetry.

An asymmetry of formal power or positional authority deals with problems caused by differences in the chain of command or power hierarchy. Birnbaum (1988) discusses the forms of authority found on campus, the administrative authority of the administration and the professional authority of the faculty. Altbach (2005) writes about the movement in higher education toward an administrative culture and estate (see also Kerr 1972). Gumport and Pusser (1995) show evidence of bureaucratic accretion, the relative growth of administrative positions at a rate that outstrips the growth of faculty on campus. These suggestions alone would perhaps create a growing asymmetry between faculty and administrators. However, given the findings of Caboni, Fleming, Hodum, and Bray, it is clear that although there is a burgeoning administrative culture, it is not one that can be covered with a single stroke of normative expectation or one code of conduct. Instead, there exist multiple subcultures, consistent with and in some ways paralleling the cosmopolitan and local (Gouldner 1957) division among faculty. Administrators too have their affiliation to specialization as well as their affiliation to institution, and thus codes for areas like fund-raising and admissions administrators have been developed and should continue to be revisited and refined.

With a differential of subcultures within administration, the asymmetrical focus rests upon positional authority with many layers to it. However, it would be remiss to consider all administrative culture as driven by positional power. The recent case of Penn State University and the power wielded by not only upper-level administrators but by those in athletics and the football program specifically (Freeh, Sporkin, and Sullivan, 2012), shows clearly that power can become affiliated with a specific area of campus function or administration. Unfortunately, the Penn State case also all too clearly illustrates the vulnerabilities inherent in the system, and the need to protect those not in places of power. Freeh, Sporkin, and Sullivan (2012) call on the Penn State administration to, among other things, develop a stronger sense of accountability and to develop ethics-based decision making as part of their culture, something postulated directly in the first tenet in

Fleming's empirically derived code for presidents. Freeh, Sporkin, and Sullivan (2012) also call for greater delineation of administrative roles and powers to ensure there is not too much power or expectation placed in or upon the president or other upper-level administrators; the confusion of higher education administrative roles is a constant in much of the scholarly literature (Fleming, chapter 2; Wolverton, Wolverton, and Gmelch 1999).

Thus, positional power asymmetries are critical to consider in defining and developing codes of conduct. Based on empirically derived codes, it is clear that there are inherent vulnerabilities of the student in dealing with faculty or administrators (poor mentoring can lead to lessened professional opportunities, immoral behavior can lead to long-term issues, and so forth) (see Proper and Lyken-Segosebe et al. in chapters 6 and 7); just as faculty can suffer from inappropriate behaviors of administrators (for instance, loss of ability to advance in one's career; see Bray, chapter 3). Donors can suffer from fund-raiser behavior (inappropriate use of funds or representation to donors; Caboni, chapter 5); prospective students and parents can face challenges from poor conduct of an admissions officer (such as lack of opportunity, wasted effort and resources; Hodum, chapter 4); and multiple stakeholders can bear the brunt of poor presidential behavior (Fleming, chapter 2). In some cases given power and positional authority differentials, the vulnerabilities include reprisals for any behavior those in higher levels of command find undesirable, including disagreement or discord.

Professional authority or expertise is often the bailiwick of faculty control. Much of the discussion of asymmetry focuses upon the balance between faculty of junior versus senior rank. Those with tenure and full-professor title have established their professional authority and can use that power to bring more junior colleagues in line. Particularly as that professional expertise gives senior faculty say in promotion and tenure decisions, professional authority gives senior faculty the ability to decide whom to bring to the institution, what behavior to reward, and what work they find valuable. However, there are critical asymmetries and vulnerabilities in faculty–student relationships as well. Proper (chapter 6) not only speaks to faculty teaching graduate students, but her empirically based tenets note specifically the power differential that exists and just how much power a faculty member, particularly a chair, has. As they mentor students who often are earning the same degree as they themselves have, faculty have expertise authority to decide which student products are considered meritorious or not.

Issues and Recommendations to Address Asymmetries and Vulnerabilities

The tenets of the codes of conduct proposed in the chapters of this volume emerged from empirically derived normative structures. Given that these norms proscribe behaviors, violations of the tenets of these various codes constitute acts of wrongdoing. Because "norms and behavior are never perfectly correlated" (Zuckerman 1988, 516), we can anticipate some wrongdoing by occupants of the critical role positions of the presidency, academic deanship, admissions officers, fund-raising professionals, and college and university faculty members. The asymmetries and vulnerabilities noted earlier highlight the importance of protecting stakeholders from violations of these codes. As a consequence, mechanisms of social control of wrongdoing must exist in colleges and universities to safeguard the welfare of the various clients served. Deterrence, detection, and sanctioning of wrongdoing stand as important mechanisms of social control (Zuckerman 1988).

Each of these mechanisms of social control presents issues that require institutional action. Codes of conduct play a central role in each of these mechanisms. However, the institutional promulgation of codes of conduct stands as particularly important to the deterrence and detection of wrongdoing. Codes for administrative positions and codes for undergraduate and graduate college teaching constitute two categories of codes colleges and universities should develop.

However, a key issue confronting colleges and universities choosing to publicize codes of conduct concerns whether to develop a single code for administrative positions or separate codes for the presidency, academic deans, admissions officers and fund-raising professionals. A single code would require a synthesis of the total of thirty-two tenets advanced for these positions by the authors of the first five chapters of this volume—a synthesis into a more general set of tenets that cut across these administrative roles. Given this challenge and our discussion of the variegation and dissensus that exists, we recommend that *separate codes of conduct for the presidency, academic deans, admissions officers, and fund-raising professional should be publicly promulgated*. We make this recommendation for two reasons. First, a synthesis of the thirty-two tenets might produce tenets so general that ambiguity surrounding acts of wrongdoing would result. Such ambiguity would make both deterrence and detection difficult. Second, each of the thirty-two tenets emerged from empirically derived normative patterns that pertain to a given administrative position. A single code would attenuate the robust empirical foundation upon which the tenets posited for each administrative position rest.

For these same reasons, we also recommend that *separate codes of conduct be publicly promulgated for undergraduate teaching and graduate teaching and mentoring*. Teaching-oriented undergraduate colleges and universities would develop only codes of conduct for undergraduate college teaching. The ten tenets proposed by Braxton and Bayer (2004) and described in the study conducted by Lyken-Segosebe, Min, and Braxton in chapter 7 provides the basis for a code of conduct for undergraduate college teaching, whereas a code of conduct for graduate teaching and mentoring could include the six tenets delineated by Proper in chapter 6.

Another issue centers on how individuals learn the tenets of the codes of conduct germane to them. Deterrence and detection of wrongdoing require knowledge of the tenets of codes of conduct for these administrative positions. We contend that knowledge of the tenets of codes of conduct comes from using adherence to such tenets as an expectation for role performance. Accordingly, we recommend that *adherence to the tenets of codes of conduct be used as a criterion for the assessment of administrative role performance for such decisions as annual salary adjustments, reappointment, and promotion.*

Likewise, knowledge of the tenets of codes of conduct for undergraduate teaching and graduate teaching and mentoring are important to the deterrence and detection of faculty violations of these tenets. We recommend that *orientation programs for new faculty members include a session on the codes of conduct for undergraduate and graduate teaching.* Of course, only universities that award doctoral degrees would include in such a session the code of conduct for graduate teaching and mentoring. We also recommend that *adherence to the tenets of either of these two teaching centered codes of conduct be used as a criterion for the assessment of professorial role performance for use in annual salary adjustments, reappointment, tenure, and promotion decisions.*

The detection of administrative or teaching wrongdoing raises a key question requiring resolution: How do individuals who personally observe acts of teaching or administrative wrongdoing report such incidents? The likelihood of detection is unlikely without such reports. To address this critical issue of detection, we recommend that *colleges and universities should create administrative and teaching integrity committees to handle reports of administrative or teaching improprieties.* Administrative integrity committees should develop mechanisms for clients external to the institution to report violations of tenets of codes of conduct. Such external clients include prospective donors, prospective students, and their parents. Following the recommendation of Braxton, Proper, and Bayer (2011), universities could also form subcommittees for teaching, one for undergraduate teaching and the other for graduate teaching and mentoring. Both types of committees should develop procedures that ensure confidentiality for both the accused and the accuser.

The recommendation of sanctions for wrongdoing constitutes a possible responsibility for both administrative and teaching integrity committees. The public display of possible sanctions serves the social control mechanisms of deterrence and sanctioning. Sanctions deter wrongdoing if known and communicated (Ben-Yehuda 1985; Tittle 1980). The delineation of possible sanctions presents an issue requiring institutional action. Accordingly, *we recommend that colleges and universities that publicly transmit administrative and teaching codes of conduct should also publicly display a range of possible sanctions that may be meted out for violating tenets of codes of conduct.* Franke (2002) offers sanctions that could be meted out for administrative transgressions as well as teaching improprieties. These possible sanctions include warning or reprimanding the individual, public censure of the offending individual, no salary increase or reduction in salary for the individual, or requiring that the offending individual undergo counseling or workshop attendance. Termination of the employment of the offending administrator or faculty member stands as the most severe of possible sanctions. The sanction selected depends on the harm done to the client by the violation of a tenet or tenets of codes of conduct as well as the frequency of such violations by the offending individual. Put differently, is a given act an isolated incident or is a part of a pattern of frequent tenet violation? We concur with the assertion of Braxton and Bayer (2004) that the greater the harm and the more pervasive the wrongdoing, the greater the severity of the sanction recommended.

Conclusion

Empirically derived codes of conduct have the opportunity to help resolve role ambiguity, to make clear across stakeholder groups the expectations of how administrators and faculty should carry out their roles, and to clarify how campus stakeholders should report violations of specific forms of wrongdoing. Given recently seen failures to report wrongdoing, we believe strongly in the importance of making codes for conduct publicly available and making them a critical part of promotion and salary decisions.

To remain timely and targeted, these codes of conduct must be empirically derived from across campuses and stakeholder groups but be focused at each level and area of administration as well as at the graduate and undergraduate faculty levels. These codes must also be periodically updated, at phases of no longer than every decade, to remain relevant. The current rate of change in higher education may ultimately dictate an even faster reevaluation of codes, and as yet unforeseen areas may also needs codes to be developed in the intervening time. Further work also needs to be done looking across institutional types to identify any profound differences in expectations, particularly among administrative functions. With a sustained focus on empirically derived tenets for codes of conduct, a more ethical and less ambiguous culture can be developed and maintained.

References

Altbach, P. G. 2005. "Patterns in American Higher Education Development." In *American Higher Education in the Twenty-First Century: Social, Political, and Economic Challenges,* 2nd ed., edited by P. G. Altbach, R. O. Berdahl, and P. J. Gumport. Baltimore: Johns Hopkins University Press.

American Educational Research Association. 2011. *Code of Ethics.* http://www.aera.net/Portals/38/docs/About_AERA/CodeOfEthics(1).pdf.

Ben-Yehuda, N. 1985. *Deviance and Moral Boundaries.* Chicago: University of Chicago Press.

Birnbaum, R. 1988. *How Colleges Work: The Cybernetics of Academic Organization and Leadership.* San Francisco: Jossey-Bass.

Braxton, J. M., and A. E. Bayer, 1999. *Faculty Misconduct in Collegiate Teaching.* Baltimore: Johns Hopkins University Press.

Braxton, J. M., and A. E. Bayer. 2004. "Toward a Code of Conduct for Undergraduate Teaching." In *Addressing Faculty and Student Classroom Improprieties,* New Directions for Teaching and Learning, no. 99, edited by J. M Braxton and A. E. Bayer, 47–55. San Francisco: Jossey-Bass.

Braxton, J. M., E. Proper, and A. E. Bayer. 2011. *Professors Behaving Badly: Faculty Misconduct in Graduate Education.* Baltimore: Johns Hopkins University Press.

Bray, N. J. 2008. "Proscriptive Norms for Academic Deans: Comparing Faculty Expectations across Institutional and Disciplinary Boundaries." *Journal of Higher Education* 79(6): 692–721.

Franke, A. 2002, March 22. "Faculty Misconduct, Discipline, and Dismissal." Paper presented at the Annual Meeting of the National Association of College and University Attorneys, New Orleans, LA.

Freeh, Sporkin, and Sullivan, LLC. 2012. *Report of the Special Investigative Counsel Regarding the Actions of the Pennsylvania State University Related to the Child Sexual Abuse Committed by Gerald A. Sandusky.* http://www.thefreehreportonpsu.com/REPORT_FINAL_071212.pdf.

Gouldner, A. W. 1957. "Cosmopolitans and Locals: Toward an Analysis of Latent Social Roles." *Administrative Science Quarterly* 2(3): 281–306.

Gumport, P., and B. Pusser. 1995. "A Case of Bureaucratic Accretion: Context and Consequences." *Journal of Higher Education* 66(5): 493–520.

Kerr, C. 1972. "The Administration of Higher Education in an Era of Change and Conflict." Speech presented as the First David D. Henry Lecture, University of Illinois at Urbana-Champaign. ERIC Document Reproduction Service No. ED 095 726.

Kerr, C. 1986. "Agenda for Higher Education: Retrospect and Prospect." Paper presented to the Annual Meeting of the Southern Regional Education Board, Atlanta, GA.

Tittle, C. 1980. *Sanctions and Social Deviance: The Question of Deterrence.* New York: Praeger.

Vaughan, G. B. 1992. "Leaders on a Tightrope: The Risks and Tensions of Community College Leaders." In G. B. Vaughan and Associates, *Dilemmas of Leadership: Decision Making and Ethics in the Community College.* San Francisco: Jossey-Bass.

Volkwein, J. F. 1999. "The Four Faces of Institutional Research." In *What Is Institutional Research All About? A Critical and Comprehensive Assessment of the Profession,* New Directions for Institutional Research, no. 104, edited by J. F. Volkwein, 9–19. San Francisco: Jossey-Bass.

Wolverton, M., M. L. Wolverton, and W. H. Gmelch. 1999. "The Impact of Role Conflict and Ambiguity on Academic Deans." *Journal of Higher Education* 70: 80–106.

Zuckerman, H. 1988. "The Sociology of Science." In *Handbook of Sociology,* edited by N. Smelser. Thousand Oaks, CA: Sage Publications.

Zusman, A. 2005. "Challenges Facing Higher Education in the Twenty-First Century." In *American Higher Education in the Twenty-First Century: Social, Political, and Economic Challenges,* 2nd ed., edited by P. G. Altbach, R. O. Berdahl, and P. J. Gumport. Baltimore: Johns Hopkins University Press.

NATHANIEL J. BRAY *is an associate professor and program coordinator in Higher Education Administration at the University of Alabama. His research interests include normative structures for academic administrators, sociology of higher education, and student issues across higher education.*

JOHN M. BRAXTON *is professor of education in the Higher Education Leadership and Policy Program at Peabody College of Vanderbilt University. Professor Braxton's scholarly interests include social control in academia with a particular focus on codes of conduct; norms; and the deterrence, detection, and sanctioning of violations of codes and norms.*

INDEX

ORDER FORM SUBSCRIPTION AND SINGLE ISSUES

DISCOUNTED BACK ISSUES:

Use this form to receive 20% off all back issues of *New Directions for Higher Education*.
All single issues priced at **$23.20** (normally $29.00)

TITLE	ISSUE NO.	ISBN

Call 888-378-2537 or see mailing instructions below. When calling, mention the promotional code JBNND to receive your discount. For a complete list of issues, please visit www.josseybass.com/go/ndhe

SUBSCRIPTIONS: (1 YEAR, 4 ISSUES)

☐ New Order   ☐ Renewal

U.S.	☐ Individual: $89	☐ Institutional: $292
CANADA/MEXICO	☐ Individual: $89	☐ Institutional: $332
ALL OTHERS	☐ Individual: $113	☐ Institutional: $366

Call 888-378-2537 or see mailing and pricing instructions below.
Online subscriptions are available at www.onlinelibrary.wiley.com

ORDER TOTALS:

Issue / Subscription Amount: $ _____

Shipping Amount: $ _____
(for single issues only – subscription prices include shipping)

Total Amount: $ _____

SHIPPING CHARGES:

First Item	$6.00
Each Add'l Item	$2.00

(No sales tax for U.S. subscriptions. Canadian residents, add GST for subscription orders. Individual rate subscriptions must be paid by personal check or credit card. Individual rate subscriptions may not be resold as library copies.)

BILLING & SHIPPING INFORMATION:

☐ **PAYMENT ENCLOSED:** *(U.S. check or money order only. All payments must be in U.S. dollars.)*

☐ **CREDIT CARD:**   ☐ VISA   ☐ MC   ☐ AMEX

Card number _____ Exp. Date _____

Card Holder Name _____ Card Issue # _____

Signature _____ Day Phone _____

☐ **BILL ME:** *(U.S. institutional orders only. Purchase order required.)*

Purchase order # _____
Federal Tax ID 13559302 • GST 89102-8052

Name _____

Address _____

Phone _____ E-mail _____

Copy or detach page and send to: **John Wiley & Sons, One Montgomery Street, Suite 1200, San Francisco, CA 94104-4594**

Order Form can also be faxed to: **888-481-2665**

PROMO JBNND

Statement of Ownership

Statement of Ownership, Management, and Circulation (required by 39 U.S.C. 3685), filed on OCTOBER 1, 2012 for NEW DIRECTIONS FOR HIGHER EDUCATION (Publication No. 0271-0560), published Quarterly for an annual subscription price of $89 at Wiley Subscription Services, Inc., at Jossey-Bass, One Montgomery St., Suite 1200, San Francisco, CA 94104-4594.

The names and complete mailing addresses of the Publisher, Editor, and Managing Editor are: Publisher, Wiley Subscription Services, Inc., A Wiley Company at San Francisco, One Montgomery St., Suite 1200, San Francisco, CA 94104-4594; Editor, Betsy Barefoot EdD, Gardner Inst. for Excellence in Undergrad. Education, Box 72, Brevard, NC 28712; Managing Editor, None,   . Contact Person: Joe Schuman; Telephone: 415-782-3232.

NEW DIRECTIONS FOR HIGHER EDUCATION is a publication owned by Wiley Subscription Services, Inc., 111 River St., Hoboken, NJ 07030. The known bondholders, mortgagees, and other security holders owning or holding 1% or more of total amount of bonds, mortgages, or other securities are (see list).

	Average No. Copies Each Issue During Preceding 12 Months	No. Copies Of Single Issue Published Nearest To Filing Date (Summer 2012)
15a. Total number of copies (net press run)	764	738
15b. Legitimate paid and/or requested distribution (by mail and outside mail)		
15b(1). Individual paid/requested mail subscriptions stated on PS form 3541 (include direct written request from recipient, telemarketing, and Internet requests from recipient, paid subscriptions including nominal rate subscriptions, advertiser's proof copies, and exchange copies)	294	268
15b(2). Copies requested by employers for distribution to employees by name or position, stated on PS form 3541	0	0
15b(3). Sales through dealers and carriers, street vendors, counter sales, and other paid or requested distribution outside USPS	0	0
15b(4). Requested copies distributed by other mail classes through USPS	0	0
15c. Total paid and/or requested circulation (sum of 15b(1), (2), (3), and (4))	294	268
15d. Nonrequested distribution (by mail and outside mail)		
15d(1). Outside county nonrequested copies stated on PS form 3541	26	19
15d(2). In-county nonrequested copies stated on PS form 3541	0	0
15d(3). Nonrequested copies distributed through the USPS by other classes of mail	0	0
15d(4). Nonrequested copies distributed outside the mail	0	0
15e. Total nonrequested distribution (sum of 15d(1), (2), (3), and (4))	26	19
15f. Total distribution (sum of 15c and 15e)	320	287
15g. Copies not distributed	444	451
15h. Total (sum of 15f and 15g)	764	738
15i. Percent paid and/or requested circulation (15c divided by 15f times 100)	92%	93.3%

I certify that all information furnished on this form is true and complete. I understand that anyone who furnishes false or misleading information on this form or who omits material or information requested on this form may be subject to criminal sanctions (including fines and imprisonment) and/or civil sanctions (including civil penalties).

Statement of Ownership will be printed in the Winter 2012 issue of this publication.

(signed) Susan E. Lewis, VP & Publisher-Periodicals

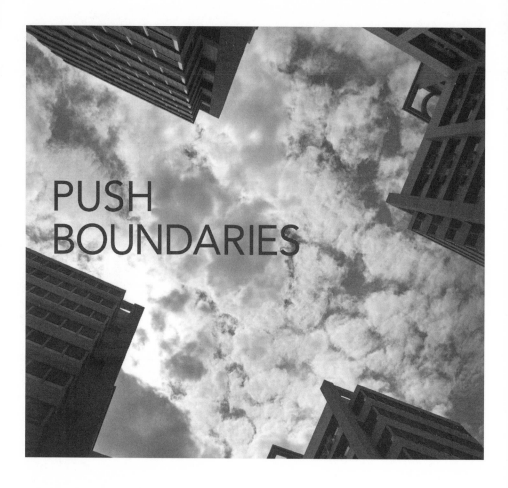